Watercolor Painting

Watercolor

Yar G. Chomicky

The Pennsylvania State University

MEDIA, METHODS, and MATERIALS

PRENTICE-HALL, INC., ENGLEWOOD CLIFFS, NEW JERSEY

Watercolor Painting

MEDIA, METHODS, and MATERIALS, by Yar G. Chomicky

Library of Congress Catalog Card Number: 68–12553

Printed in the United States of America

Current Printing (Last Digit):

10   9   8   7   6   5   4   3

PRENTICE-HALL INTERNATIONAL, Inc., *London*
PRENTICE-HALL OF AUSTRALIA, Pty. Ltd., *Sydney*
PRENTICE-HALL OF CANADA, Ltd., *Toronto*
PRENTICE-HALL OF INDIA Private Ltd., *New Delhi*
PRENTICE-HALL OF JAPAN, Inc., *Tokyo*

Acknowledgments

Many people gave of themselves in the
preparation of this book. The assistances were numerous,
and perhaps beyond acknowledgment on every
count. Old friends and strangers become friends offered
their interests, understandings, and their talents
or properties—and all of these I gratefully sought and
accepted, knowing the need beyond myself for
the enrichment of my topics. And for that part which
I could contribute, my thanks go to former
teachers who, differing in their academic allegiances,
provided a regard for completeness of knowledge
and a sense of creative respect. This last might not have
been as fully comprehended without the
privilege of association with the late Viktor Lowenfeld
at The Pennsylvania State University.

Invaluable were the favors of my dear friends Albert Christ-Janer, Bill Coleman, Chen Chi, and Edward L. Mattil. It was Mr. Christ-Janer who helped locate certain works, which in turn led to fruitful correspondences with artists and museum directors, among them Mr. John Gordon, Curator, The Whitney Museum of American Art. To Mr. Coleman, I am indebted for the fine photography which reveals his grasp of the key features represented in the demonstration series. An awakening of interest in oriental methods came from Mr. Chen. And, from Mr. Mattil, a close colleague of many years, came encouragement and other considerations.

As part of this writing experience, I shall always have special remembrances for the many gallery directors who made me feel most welcome in giving access to their files. Miss Antoinette Kraushaar and Mr. John Marin, Jr., were particularly gracious. And singularly significant was the intrepid persistence of Mr. James M. Guiher, of Prentice-Hall, Inc., who asserted real confidence in my project, even after its loss in an air crash from which he and all passengers miraculously escaped. And my thanks to Miss Sandra Houser for her many hours of correspondence and typing of the manuscript. Also my appreciation is due those whose contributions appear throughout the book.

Not as apparent, but of utmost advantage was the quiet support and strength maintained throughout by Barbara, my wife. My children, too, Colm, Amy, and Lisa, were indulgent, but only some of the time, which is as it should have been.

Contents

1

Introduction

There is a watercolor medium for everyone.
Each of the several related watercolor media is sufficiently
diverse in character to provide a different avenue
to satisfying painting experience. Means and qualities
can be matched to individual temperaments.

Transparent watercolor is versatile, elusive, and alluring.
More predictable and amenable are the opaque
watercolor vehicles, among which *gouache* enjoys
widespread favor, with casein tempera its closest rival.
Exquisitely beautiful, egg tempera is pleasurable
to the eye and to the hand. Pastel, surprisingly perhaps,
also qualifies as a watercolor. The same is true of
the inks. And, for the more restless and venturesome,
the latest in synthetic emulsions offers new sets
of characteristics and the potentialities of new visions.

Finally, mixed-media offer even more expanded possibilities than are provided by even the most venturesome single medium.

In this volume, media, procedures, and general practices are examined as products of tradition. The intent is to establish a base of information broad enough to help the learner orient himself to the kinds of problems and solutions to be expected with each medium, making it possible for the beginner to start with more knowledge and with more sophisticated sets of criteria by which efforts might be compared and progress noted. However, unless mere duplication in every detail of the descriptions and instructions included here is avoided, results are apt to be static, sterile, and stereotyped. Too much dependence upon formalities can prove disastrous. Fortunately, in each of us there is at least enough strength of peculiarity in want of assertion to counteract technical impositions. In the end, the sense of craft instilled by an enlarged knowledge of technique may not be enough, unless it is influenced and sustained by a parallel growth of capacity to personalize meaningfully. Basic methods serve best when looked upon as guides which can be revised rather than as closed systems which do not tolerate improvisation.

All visual materials were selected or developed for their instructional value. Although they demonstrate some applied principles, their primary purpose is to suggest the diversity of handling and interpretation possible. By coincidence, they also represent segments of the painting history of watercolor vehicles, but they must not be looked at as a portfolio of styles from which one can be picked as casually as an article of clothing, like the response of a young boy who, much impressed by an exhibition, was overheard to say that his next painting would be "a John Marin." The intent of the examples is to arouse insight rather than imitation.

Eventually, when media and processes are better understood, the elements of individualized technique are likely to take shape. In anticipation of change and independence, an aspiration to gear every sense and effort of the imagination to the highest level of expression and performance will result in more significant ends and means.

CHAPTER 1

The Watercolor Processes

In the strictest sense, watercolor painting refers to
the use of pigments which have gums as their binders
and which use water as a solvent. This restricted
definition prescribes a form of painting in which pigments
are used transparently and without the use of white
pigment. In an expanded definition, white pigment may
be mixed with water soluble colors resulting in
opaque characteristics, so long as water remains as the
vehicle. If the use of water as a vehicle is allowed
to be the primary qualification for watercolor processes,
pigment prepared with binders other than gums
are admitted to the water color category. The temperas,
inclusive of all emulsion preparations, as well as
various of the mixed-media combinations are thus acceptable.

Courtesy M. Knoedler and Co., Inc., New York

Artist: *WINSLOW HOMER*
Title: *Coconut Palms, Key West, 1886*
Medium: Watercolor

    A watercolor style may consist of no more than wistful suggestions of form or line. Otherwise, depending upon visual objectives, the result may be a developed system of complex manipulations and ensuing effects. A complete master of the medium, Winslow Homer employed painting treatments as he required. In this example the brushwork is unerringly controlled. Not restricted to purely descriptive detail, each stroke is fitted into an accumulation of strokes that follow the movements underlying the organization or composition of the work.

TRANSPARENT WATERCOLOR

The transparent painting method is the most capricious of all, owing to the greater amounts of water necessary to secure transparent color ranges. In applying water-diluted mixtures to a paper ground, the amount required is usually sufficient to cause a secondary water action. *This is probably the most significant observation to be made.* What must be understood is the hydraulic action of water as it affects the ground and pigment dispersal. Herein lies the key to control of transparent painting and the two basic stylistic variations associated with it.

the binder and water

Pigments are minute particles of coloring matter; when combined with a binder, each particle becomes surrounded by the binder vehicle. In this state the particles are enabled to cling to each other and to the support, or ground, as paint. The binder agent traditionally used to combine with pigments to produce water color is gum arabic; although gum Senegal has replaced gum arabic to a great extent largely because of limited world supply of the latter. Actually gum Senegal is better. Somewhat less soluble in water, gum Senegal is less prone to washes and other overpainting techniques.

Gums are soluble in water. When water is added to a water color the adhered pigment particles separate and become suspended in the water body while the adhesive property of the gum normally is not greatly diminished. Thereafter, when water has evaporated from the support, the pigment grains adhere themselves to the ground. This jointure is not permanent however.

Watercolor paint layers are vulnerable to the action of any subsequent contacts with water. For this reason when overlayers are applied, care should be taken not to disturb the underpainting. An underlayer should be completely dry before another is superimposed, and for clear, vibrant coloration no given area should be covered with more than three overlays. Soft-haired brushes are advised whenever overpainting is attempted. This same feature of solubility, we should note, is also the basis for a painting technique which largely consists of the washing away of pigment layers. The regaining of lightened effects, including highlights, is similarly achieved.

The continual tendency of water to dissolve gum binders and to erode paint layers can be minimized. To maintain adhesive strength, the painting water is frequently fortified with adhesive materials A supplementary mixture regarded as suitable is one consisting of gum arabic (or gum Senegal), glycerine, and alcohol, in a basic ratio of three parts gum to one part glycerine to which a small quantity of grain alcohol is added after the gum and glycerine have been dissolved in warm water. In place of this mixture, commonplace rock candy, honey—and even beer—are convenient and effective additives. Improved manipulations and visual results are immediate benefits. Mixtures on the palette remain tractable longer than when wetted with water by itself. Greater brilliance and depth of color also result when underlayers are able to remain least altered by water in overlayer mixtures.

Any additional comments about water as a medium may seem unnecessary, yet one should not take too much for granted. The water must be clean and chemically inert. Water which is known to carry sulphides, traces of detergents, or other impurities should be avoided. Naturally soft waters, such as from pure springs and rain water, are best. Modern tap-water is generally safe, but whenever doubts exist, distilled water is recommended. These points will be resumed in greater detail in a later section.

the support and water

Earlier it was noted that water exerts an action when deposited upon paper. It penetrates the fibers of paper, soaking and swelling them as it spreads and moistens a larger area before coming to a stop. When a brushload of moistened pigment is introduced onto a freshly wetted paper, the free pigment particles will distribute themselves in the direction taken by the water. They are borne along by its movements. This relationship of free water, released pigment, and absorbing ground defines the underlying differences between the now most universal transparent painting approaches, *wet-on-dry* and *wet-in-wet*.

Artist: *THOMAS MORAN*
Title: *Cliffs of Ecclesbourne near Hastings*
Medium: Pencil, wash, and Chinese white

This watercolor by Thomas Moran, one of America's foremost nineteenth-century artists, corresponds quite closely to the simple and direct wash approach described by Francis Nicholson as First Process. The neutral tint in this example was a gray-green, a color much like the patina on bronze sculpture. The touches, or fuller-bodied indications, by which details were developed, depend here upon pencil and Chinese white.

In no other painting process is the physical effect of the medium on the support more critical. The variations in moisture content which can be infused are many. The painter must come to know what degrees of ground wetness will result in the various characteristic sets of paint effects. And in no other painting situation is the support incorporated more as an inseparable component in the intermixing of pigments. The white of admixtures, it should be stressed, is provided by utilizing the whiteness of the support.

WET-ON-DRY PAINTING

The principle of wet-on-dry painting involves the limited use of water. When a work in this manner is begun, the support is in a dry stage. Thereafter time is allowed for each fresh paint layer to dry as the painting progresses through phases from the first localizing underpainting to successive overlays and finally to the last indications of detailings. The method is most often encountered in the production of works which require greatly controlled treatment of subject matter, precisely or accurately.

Hard-edge painting is the dominant manipulative characteristic of the wet-on-dry method; lines and areas are contained within definite boundaries—which is not to say that wash effects are eliminated completely. They can be and are used in the wet-on-dry context, provided that the usual drying sequences are dominant.

An extreme form of virtually waterless painting is the *dry-brush* method. In this instance not only is the support kept dry but the brush itself is not fully wetted. The only moisture carried by the brush is the minimal amount used in keeping the pigments moistened. The effect obtained is an indistinct and somewhat erratic hatching directly resulting from the dragging of the brush. The "tooth," or grain, of the paper contributes to this appearance. Dry-brush may be a legitimate technique when used alone, but it is also useful at any time to produce textural treatments or to "build-up" details of a painting. The use of stiff brushes with bristles somewhat spread is one type of the dry-brush technique. In all dry-brush work, the more the pigments are kept undiluted, the greater their covering power will be.

WET-ON-DRY EFFECTS

In wet-on-dry painting single-stroke brushwork on a perfectly dry surface will remain intact and unaffected by the ground. The shape, the thickness, the direction or path taken by a stroke, and the kind of tool executing it remain recognizable. Linear and calligraphic qualities are incipient to dry and relatively dry paper supports. A point to remember, however, is that once water begins to be introduced in any form to the support, wet-on-wet conditions begin to enter the painting problem.

1. Loaded to its capacity, an oriental brush—or hair pen—has been pulled, pressed, and twirled over an area of dry paper. The hairs have been parted into more than one tip, purely for the sake of demonstrating one very simple modification. The amounts of water within the bounds of the lines vary from heavy deposits held by surface tension to lighter and almost dry indications where the brush's charge has dissipated itself.

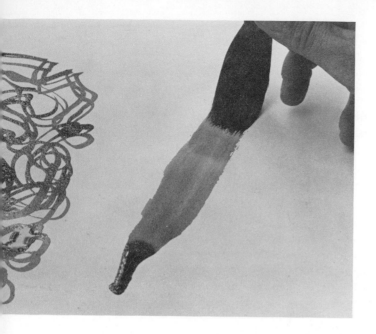

2. Leaving the first area, where not all of the water has been imbibed by the paper as yet, a new stroke has been made. Beginning with a deliberately prolonged touching of just the tip to the surface, the brush was pulled with gradual increase of pressure to broaden the line and to affect a wider area. Although this illustration simply demonstrates a means of gradation of color, the conditions of a wet ground on a small scale have entered the picture.

3. To suggest improvisation and to contrast a dry ground with a wet one in close proximity, ink discharged from a bottle stopper is randomly directed over the wet stroke and neighboring areas. Within the body of the brush stroke, the pen line is slightly diffused, while outside it the remaining lines are typically wet-on-dry: crisp, dark, held by surface tension.

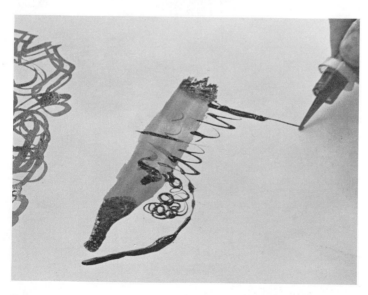

4.   In this illustration more ink lines have been brought into play to add to the graphic activity. With a brush, a small *hake* (flat) lightly loaded with clear water is made to pass across a still fresh ink line. Some of the ink is picked up and trails with the stroke. When a line or an edge of a painted area is made to spread by wetting the adjacent surface, the affected indication is said to have been "softened off."

5.   The device of "softening off" is employed here to intermix colors, as a fresh ink stroke and watercolor in place of clear water are introduced. Heavy with ink, the stroke quickly mingles with the pigment into another blending.

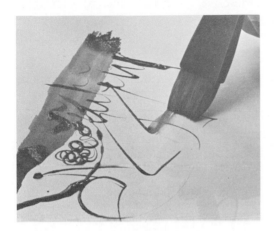 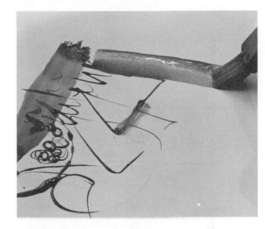

6.   The exploration is continued. Much of the work in ink is still fresh, suggesting, perhaps, the further development of "softening off" treatments.

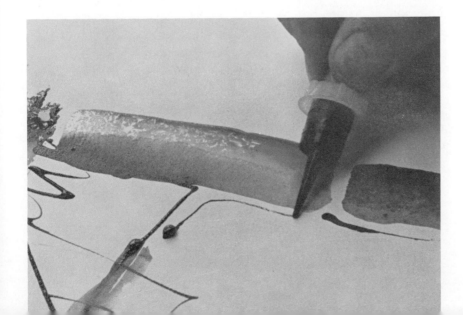

**origin of
wet-on-dry
methods**

The wet-on-dry principle is often known as the English method. Highly developed toward the close of the eighteenth century, the generalized approach consisted of four variations, known as the "processes in coloring" and designated simply as the *First Process*, the *Second Process*, the *Third Process*, and the *Fourth Process*. These processes are generic to current practices and have been restated in various ways since the eighteenth century. The new terms which have arisen, however, describe essentially the same instructions and observations. *Wet-on-dry*, for example, is a latter-day terminology.

Traditional practices are not necessarily to be shunned and condemned as stultifying to creative results. Any practice of any moment —yesterday, now, and hence—which is not held to strict limits can be redefined and converted into additional advantages. The processes of painting note and call attention to the behavior of materials and other physical conditions, and the knowledge thus gained benefits the development of facility and dexterity. But this same capacity becomes useless if it becomes a mechanical and repetitious demonstration of skill without thought. The plea for the subordination of means to ends is not new nor is it likely to be stilled. Two centuries ago Francis Nicholson attempted to make the same point, condemning "the copyist" and "that careless kind of practice in which the mind has not a principal share." His contemporary and rival of sorts, Alexander Cozens, added that there was not only too much imitation of nature but too much direct copying of other artists' works also. It is difficult to imagine that any watercolor can be copied exactly or that such efforts were ever dared.

A review of the basic differences and functions of the four prototype processes can assist in understanding the value of organizing an approach to painting problems. In this instance, these classic methods imply that a solution can begin from at least one of four directions, that it may be with the simplest of means or it may be a complex composite of several strategies.

Originally the processes to be described here appeared as step-by-step instructions for the painting of landscapes. The landscape references will be eliminated where possible in favor of generalizations which might serve a greater number of circumstances.

SOME OF THE PARAPHERNALIA

Reading diagonally from left to right, top row: Red sable brushes, Nos. 6, 8, 12; common hair pen; Shodo hokoku writing brushes, jumbo, large, medium; hake, small, wide; water container and hair dryer. Bottom row: India ink, odd pens; baked enamel metal palette, and tube colors; semi-moist panned pigments from Japan; paper toweling and sponge.

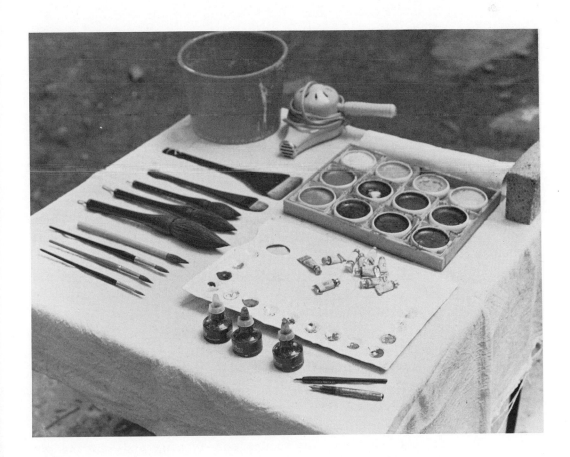

THE FIRST PROCESS

Nicholson calls this the easiest and, indeed, it is the simplest. It is seldom encountered today, yet it can be an excellent way of initiation to watercolor painting. Drawing, wash build-up, the development of forms and advancement to detail are some of the features obtainable with the least of complication.

The First Process is, in fact, a *grisaille* method, involving the establishing of the light and dark areas with a series of gray washes. Over these follow washes of warm and cool colors and, for detailings, touches of less dilute mixtures. Nicholson observes that the results often resemble tinted prints, which is more probably the fault of his description than of the capability of the medium, for as in Nicholson's account, there is too defined an outline drawing at the outset, a tendency to tint rather than to paint intrudes. This is also frequently true when watercolors occur with predominantly pen and ink delineations. In either situation, it is helpful to recognize that aids can sometimes prove more restraining than beneficial.

The gray watercolor mixture in this process is a *neutral tint*. The commercially prepared India ink which is identified as a neutral tint may be used, but the watercolor combinations that are mixed in the studio are a bit more subtle and appealing in color gradations. India inks are not stable. A *neutral tint* is a mixture of any red watercolor with blue which tends toward purple. Indigo and Indian red is one combination; another is indigo and light red, or Venetian red. Both are permanent and reliable. Less permanent, but worth the risk all the same, are the handsome pearly grays produced when indigo, lake, and yellow, or burnt Sienna are brought together. A little experimentation with substitutes for lake is another alternative.

In the indigo and Indian red mixture, the Indian red separates quickly because of its greater weight. For this reason the mixture should contain considerably more Indian red than is required when other reds are used. The pigments should be mixed in a saucer in a quantity greater than that required with other reds; the top liquid is then poured off to be used as the tint. Light red does not subside as does Indian red. The combination of indigo and light red produces a greenish gray tint because light red inclines toward orange rather than toward purple.

Experimentation with other reds in combination with blues other than indigo can result in more kinds of grays. Ground charcoal and gum water is another way of making a neutral tint. It provides a useful blue-black mixture. These different hued tints may be used together to produce unusual and subtle variations. Whatever the ingredients, however, neutral tints should be prudently diluted and mixed in a quantity sufficient to last at least through the intervals of paintings. Saucers are suitable containers. If containers having air-tight lids are used, greater quantities can be pre-mixed and stored until needed.

In the First Process the neutral tint accounts for three of the palette colors: a red, a blue, and a gray. Before the neutral tint is mixed, the red and the blue to be used should be prepared in lots of at least two ounces. Part of each is then poured into a third container and blended by stirring. As thin washes, each has a definite assignment from one painting stage to the next. In the landscape, for example, the blue (indigo) is applied to the sky area and through the middle distances, with allowance for cloud shapes and highlights. Later the blue is returned to assist in modeling, as a dark.

The first wash of neutral tint is through the middle ground, overlaying the blue and establishing the general silhouette of forms against the sky. Along its bottom edge, similar allowance is made for the silhouettes of foreground elements. The foreground is covered with a wash of the red, except where whites are to be retained, much as in the consideration of the sky.

At this point the painting is on its way. With local color, the design and content are blocked in. In the next phases the darks are strengthened with additional washes, forms are defined more, and detailings are carried further. More warm washes are added to the foreground, more neutral tint and blue washes to the middle, and neutral tint to the background as the last stage of painting is reached.

Completion of the painting consists of bringing color and the lights and darks to fuller strength. The foreground is treated with particular emphasis upon stronger contrasts: brighter colors and lights, richer and deeper darks. Reds, yellow, browns, and greens illuminate the foreground, blue, gray, and green washes give greater body to the darks and more substance to intermediate areas of middle distances.

The First Process should not be overlooked or underestimated. Much can be learned from giving it the benefit of trial before attempting more complex techniques. Any of the neutral tints described are also excellent drawing vehicles, generally having an advantage over inks in their range of variation.

THE SECOND PROCESS

Fuller-bodied color and less dependence upon gray washes are at the core of the Second Process. A neutral tint is employed, but only during the earlier phases and for subduing the white of the paper. Differentiation of parts and advancement of details are more directly painted in colors stronger and more intense than any of the neutral tints. The pervading grays of the First Process are supplemented by a scale of color.

Just as in the First Process, a neutral tint is prepared. Its use is confined to background planes—to the sky and distances in a landscape, for instance. From this point other colors are introduced, varying in temperature (warm and cool) and ranging from thin washes to full strength. Again, in simulating the illusion of depth, warm colors congregate in the foreground, cool colors in the background.

At the outset, with both this and the First Process, the preliminary neutral tint washes will flow more evenly if the paper is first slightly damp.

THE THIRD PROCESS

This process is begun and carried through in much the same way as described for the first and second variations. The whole painting is then washed down, or rinsed, with clear water.

Perhaps the simplest way of demonstrating the Third Process would be to rinse a painting which is completely dry and which has been carried through wash statements and heavier-bodied touches. The action of the water softens the gum binder and, if the painted surface is lightly scrubbed with a fairly wide brush (two to three inches), some pigment particles are loosened. These particles are then brushed off with additional applications of water. A steady, gentle touch and plenty of water is needed. Not all of the color is removable. In fact, the effect which remains is quite desirable. Not only are atmospheric or aerial tints improved, but a beautiful granulation is imparted to the surface of the paper. Visually, pigment and paper appear to be in more of an organic union and less like paint layers in the usual sense of covering a surface.

After the first washing, stronger coloration can be restored where desired. Some suggestions of form which result from erosion by the water may be retained or modified, according to appropriateness of the moment. Washing down may be renewed later, across the whole of the painting or in parts.

Wetting colored areas to loosen pigment is a useful way of restoring lights to darkened areas and of regaining lost highlights and renewing a degree of sparkle. Color is lifted with careful dabbing of a sponge or blotter. Enough water should be used to prevent streaking. The conditions under which lifting of pigment is possible also lend themselves to exploration of textural variations. Crumpled papers or cloth, for instance, can leave variegated linear patterns. Often such objects as rocks are expressed by wetting and lifting devices.

THE FOURTH PROCESS

The Fourth Process is a watercolor version of the glazing techniques employed in oil painting. Color clarity and transparency are the objectives, with visual preservation of the ground color the main consideration. The technique entails the physical isolation of color layers, completely or partly, by covering areas from layer to layer with some substance which will not give way when other colors are washed over it. Much like in the stopping out steps in the etching of a plate, the impervious material used is a wax preparation. Frisket preparations or rubber cement may be substituted, but they are not as reliable or as safe as wax because rubbing is required for their removal and injury to the paper is possible. Rubber cement also shows a definite tendency to yellow paper wherever there has been direct contact. You should be aware of these drawbacks so as not to be misled by the frequent recommendations of rubber cement for this and similar purposes.

The wax composition is a combination of a small quantity of whitened beeswax dissolved in oil of turpentine (distilled turpentine, and also spirit of turpentine) to which flake-white is added to provide an opaque body. The amount of flake-white is sufficient when a sample of the mixture on paper appears opaque when held up to the light; the amount of wax need be no more than enough to fix the flake-white. A quantity of turpentine which will keep the mixture dilute enough to be easily lifted and discharged by a pointed brush is sufficient. Evaporation of the turpentine is slowed if the mixture is kept in a small dish rather than spread across the surface of a saucer.

For the Fourth Process, rough grained paper is stipulated. Thin washes, Nicholson explains, will "remain lighter upon the prominent parts than between them," and "if used thicker and with less in the pencil [brush], it will drag upon the prominences, touching these only, and leaving the intermediate parts lighter." This aspect of the Fourth Process corresponds closely to what today is known as dry-brush.

The Fourth Process is divided into definite painting phases. Wash underlayers of either or both neutral tint and local colors are applied first. When taken as far as desired, the first colorings are allowed to dry. Those areas which are considered to be completed are covered with brushings of the wax composition. The turpentine evaporates quickly, and painting can be resumed until it is decided to cover more parts with wax. These steps are repeated until completion is reached. A wax covering over an entire painting is not unusual.

The removal of the wax is not difficult at all, thanks to the insolubility of gums in turpentine. The wax can be washed off without disturbing any of the work, provided that the colors have been allowed to dry. Turpentine is brushed on, and the dissolved wax is wiped off with a clean cloth, a small section at a time. This is continued until all of the colors are uncovered.

If it is decided to work more into the painting, turpentine remaining in the paper must be removed or it will act as a resist—a feature which may be of value in experiments in the area of mixed-media. Here, however, it can be a problem. The paper can be made to receive water color again if it is washed, front and back, with highly rectified spirit of wine (ethyl alcohol 84%).

The Fourth Process seems to be quite involved and is easily taken to be desirable only for the painter intent upon meticulous rendering. This may be true, but only to a point. There is no reason why freely brushed and spontaneously conceived paintings cannot incorporate these same operations.

One must take leave of this review of forerunner methods with a degree of respect for the basic knowledge which was in evidence during a period of painting which does not enjoy the best of reputation. Where sterility in the production of art occurs, the fault is less with information in common than with those who misuse it or ignore it.

WET-IN-WET PAINTING

The procedures of wet-in-wet treatment center upon the maintenance of wet conditions both in the support and in the pigment mixtures. A common error is the assumption that the paper must be saturated with water before painting begins and during all successive stages. Under such conditions, however, directive control is impossible. The saturated condition just described is, nevertheless, appropriate for some effects, but not for the whole possible range of effects. The degree of wetness can be gauged and associated with definite variations in pigment coverage. The degree of moisture may extend in a scale, therefore, from slight, through moderate, to full saturation.

In contrast to general characteristics of wet-on-dry pigment handling, wet-in-wet painting produces softened and diffused effects. If watercolors may be said to have a plasticity, it occurs under the wetter conditions. The flowing-on of pigment appears brushless and in a more organic affinity with the ground. Diffused areas and indefinite edges fall into the category of soft-edge painting.

WET-IN-WET SEQUENCE

In this photographic series the ground is overly wet, to demonstrate the dynamics and inertia of water as it affects both the support and color applied to it.

1. A well loaded brush is touched to the wet surface. Note the reflections and the swelling of the paper and wet tape along the lower edge.

2. The brush lifted away, the outline of the stroke is furry as it begins to spread. The pigment is pulled by capillary action and the direction of flow of superfluous water on the surface.

3. Without reloading, the brush is touched again to the paper, just below the first stroke. The small, dark droplet from the first stroke has begun to merge with the second.

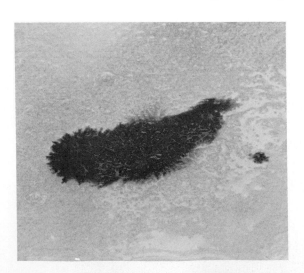
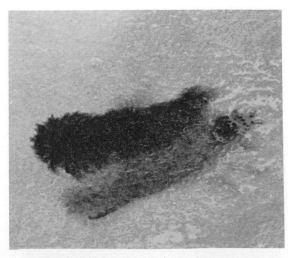

4.   While the two strokes continue to merge, a third stroke, finer than the others, trails from the brush's tip. Like the others, it diffuses very rapidly.

5.   More water is flooded to the surface and the strokes lose their identities, in part merging and otherwise flowing downward with the slight tilt of the panel.

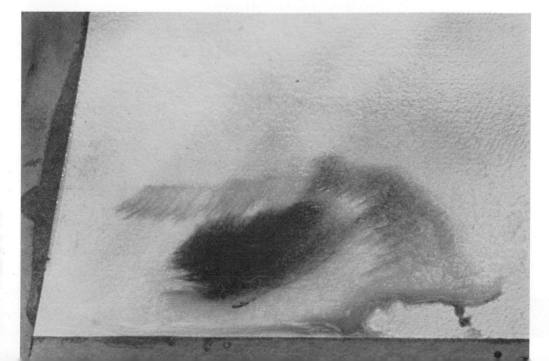

6. While the original strokes are pulled into wisps, some erratically drawn lines in India ink are brought into play. Again, spreading is very rapid.

7. The ink lines are continued into the area where the original brush strokes continue to spread.

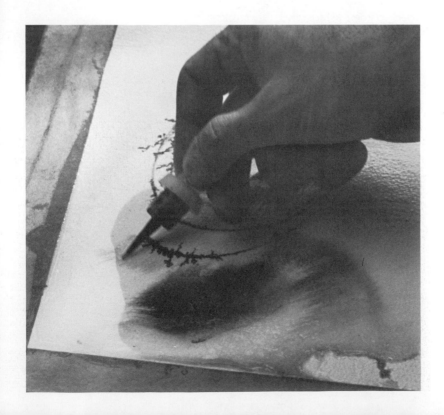

8. The ink line which passed over the old brush strokes is quickly absorbed into them. The wet paper continues to influence the original state of each drawing indication.

9. More water is added, over the ink lines only, to cause more softening of the edges and to eliminate the self-made secondary lines which crept outward from the parent lines.

10. The whole area is rinsed with a heavy dousing of water. Very little remains of the trial strokes. When wet-in-wet painting is to be used, the best condition in the ground is when it is mat, when it does not have the shine of water on the surface, as is seen in this series.

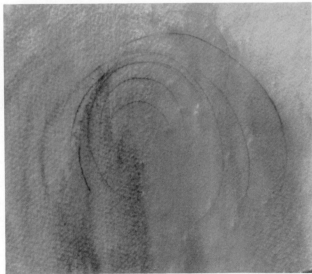

Direct wetting of the support with clear water is a self-evident means of achieving wet conditions but there are others. Less obvious is the imparting of water to the support from brushes heavily loaded with well diluted pigments. Also, the rendering of large areas and gradations is accomplished by means of washes, a flooding technique which requires a liberal quantity of water. As a result, a dry ground can become a combination of dry and wet areas at almost any point in the development of a painting—perhaps at the very beginning, with localized washes, as often happens when a typical sky rendering is the first step in a sequence of techniques. Such areas may be continued in wet-in-wet or permitted to dry as they are, to await later detailings which follow wet-on-dry and dry-brush principles.

The transparent painting approaches may be exercised singly or they may be incorporated together. Being aware of the extent to which any of them may be made to coexist in one painting is indicative of a high level of control. The acquirement of skills in this respect promotes both confidence and a spirit of daring which can carry graphic controls and achievements beyond just a preliminary mastery of fundamentals.

If any single effect could be regarded as synonymous with transparent watercolor, it would have to be the wash. A mastery of its manipulations is fundamental to full-scale management of watercolor. Washes solve a number of painting problems, and an understanding of these relationships will enable the learner to assume greater choice and authority in governing the development and progress of painting technique.

The most classic description or example of a useful wash is that which too often restricts itself to the rendering of skies. Indeed, this treatment is appropriate at times, but not for every sky in every watercolor. The real advantage of washes is that they provide a means of covering large areas fluidly, quickly, and with transparent clarity. Laying in washes as underlayers which establish forms, value, or light and dark tonalities, and other indications generalize the underlying structure or design of the painting. Beyond this point, of course, washes are continued over other washes to strengthen or modify areas as needed. In short, washes are not for skies only.

Artist: *JOHN MARIN*
Title: *Spring—Tyrol*
Medium: Watercolor

A very sensitive selection of articulate lines, restricted to wet effects, is the essence of this early work of John Marin. Its freshness is as clear and clean as Alpine air itself.

Artist: *WILLIAM THON*
Title: *Beyond Tivoli*
Medium: Watercolor

   The technique in this work employs much rinsing with water, followed by additional painting in phases. Pronounced granulation is often secured by this means, and the lightened areas are typical of wiping or lifting of paint while the surface is wet.

There are two kinds of washes, or, depending upon preference, two kinds of visual effects which are obtained by means of washes. When a large area is to be painted evenly, in one value or degree of color, an *equal* wash is employed. Its opposite is the *gradated* wash, in which variations of tones or tints make up the body of the washed area. A common example is the wash that proceeds from dark through light, as in the sky treatment mentioned here. This is a regular gradation, or "softening off," which is made by touching the edges of a painted stroke with brush and water only to extend the color beyond its first coverage. At any desired time any area of a painting may also be washed over with water only, followed by the laying in of other colors which will spread in several directions if the panel is held horizontally; or, if inclined, the spreading will descend. This operation is not clearly classified as a third type of wash, other than to be mentioned in the context of the others.

Preparation and timing are necessary to the coordinating of the steps followed in the making of washes. The procedure for the *equal* wash is as follows:

1. Mix a quantity of color which will be sufficient to cover the given space(s). This is to assure that every deposit of color will be perfectly matched; and that there will be no alteration as happens in the event that supplementary mixes are attempted to complete the operation.

2. The consistency of the mixture should be such that it will flow freely from the brush and be easily distributed upon the paper. The mixture should be diluted. The flat surface of the usual mixing palette does not hold sufficient wash in reserve. Dishes or cups might be used instead. Large brushes are preferred over smaller ones for the former's capacity to hold more color and to keep it in an equally moist state longer. The round or domed type brushes are employed, although wide, flat brushes such as the Japanese *hake* are considered to be up to the task.

3. The paper is held at a moderate tilt, the upper part raised. This position is meant to aid in the coverage of the paper or any of its parts. Beginning anywhere in the upper part and descending with more strokes, the color will run downward a little and settle or merge equally.

4. Haste should be avoided. The movement of the brush should not be faster than its ability to release color. Nor should the brush be used to a point at which its dome is exhausted. Wetness must be maintained; inconsistent wetting will result in unequal distribution of color, or inequality of tint. Attempts to rectify incomplete areas of a wash are useless. These always show as dark areas or streaks.

The *gradated* wash follows the procedure as outlined for the *equal* wash, with one difference. Coverage of area is assisted by the addition of water. The balance of water is increased as the laying in progresses, resulting in an unequally tinted wash. With the paper slightly inclined this wash is begun by pulling a full-bodied stroke of the color mixture, or connected strokes, across the top boundary of the area or shape to be filled. Before this can dry, clear water is applied along the lower edge of the stroke. The pigment is attracted to the freshly wetted part. Repeated, the color descends, becoming lighter with each dilution. The operation is facilitated if a second brush, also large, is kept in readiness for applying only the water.

MIXED METHODS

Beyond the fact that it refers to the combining of media into a single painting form, no single definition can encompass the possibilities in this technical term. Transparent and opaque watercolors are commonly paired, but, because of the license connoted, it is not surprising that other syntheses appear. Ink, chalk, crayon, polyester resins, cut paper—any and all—are introduced in company with transparent and opaque watercolor methods. Personal integrity may well be the basis for one's wisdom of choice. Outright sensationalism does not honor either materials or—what is more important—expressive truth.

THE ACCIDENT

At no time during the development of a watercolor is absolute control of the medium always possible. For one cause or another, it is more usual than rare for unexpected effects to occur. Some painters regard this feature as a defect, while others hold great faith in the accidental as a clue to more flexible techniques which reflect the true and spontaneous nature of the medium. Whenever an unanticipated effect is accepted, in either case, it is called a "happy accident."

Circumstances which contribute to the introduction of accidents are generally predictable. Differences in wetness of the support from one area to the next account for most accidents. Unintended spreading, diffusing, and intermixing of adjacent colors are typical of this condition. Other factors also may enter to influence the behavior of the paint, either by chance or design, and sometimes a combination of both. Chen Chi, the gifted American watercolorist, reported an experience which occurred while he was painting outdoors one winter's day. The freezing of water on the painting's surface created a crystalline pattern, most unusual and yet unquestionably appropriate to the needs of the moment. There are few painters who cannot contribute other examples of accidents out of their own experiences which increased their understanding of the medium. But the point to be remembered here is that sensitivity to the traits of the medium as they reveal themselves closer to their natural character can guide the painter to more effective expression and control.

One of the most intriguing departures in the development of watercolor concepts may be ascribed to an accident which, strangely enough, occurred during a period noted for its stereotyped values. Eighteenth-century England was the place, and Alexander Cozens the outspoken critic of watercolor practices. In his discourse, "A New Method of Assisting the Invention in Drawing Original Compositions of Landscape," this important figure discloses an experience which became a cornerstone for both his personal painting method and his teaching. One day, while pleading for greater originality in the landscape compositions of a gifted student, he felt his words were not conveying his generalizations satisfactorily. Disturbed and annoyed with this failure to communicate, he resorted to demonstrating current basic composition principles. Quickly, in sparing detail, he sketched the breadth of a landscape. In the few moments required for this purpose he became suddenly aware that he had oriented his design to a relationship already established by some faint stains on the paper. Intuitively he accepted this oddity and, spurred, he seized

Artist: *ESTEBAN VINCENTE*
Title: *Collage, with Pink and Yellow, 1952*
Medium: Watercolor and collage (on paper, mounted on cardboard)

Collage treatment here is beyond the ordinary, going into a complete
fusion with the paint medium. It represents pure expression and form
coming of the painting act itself.

a second sheet of paper. Rapidly, he brushed indescribable forms in a darker ink into a distribution which echoed the preceding sheet, although, to be sure, his active knowledge of composition was to some extent a curb to a purely random jotting. This he handed to the student with the instruction that he complete it, making of this suggestion a landscape. This process of reducing initial forms came to be called "blots" by Cozens and became the basis of the approach advanced in his writing.

Cozens had great faith in his means and defended the departure against the tide of criticism and ridicule which assailed his announcement. Previous to his newly established method, Cozens had publicly derided contemporary watercolor practices, contending that invention and vitality were woefully absent. In his opinion it was a low state of thinking which would condone the copying of existing works, including those of contemporaries. This habit of copying could also be found in the extreme degree to which Nature herself was slavishly imitated. The slowness and laboriousness with which watercolor paintings were executed were close to the roots of the ills enumerated by Cozens. To rid and cure landscape problems of insipidity and false precepts, he proposed diligent practicing of blots as the most immediate and releasing device. Cozens pleaded well but pleased few, and oddly enough he did not exploit his admonishments to fullest advantage in his own works. Nicholson accused Cozens of "licentiousness."

Cozens restricted the use of blots almost exclusively to sketching and planning phases preliminary to a final painting; they were to be used purely as a process of diffusing subject elements into essential forms intended to first establish a well integrated composition. Such sketches show a remarkable ease in getting to the essence of statement in a bold and striking calligraphy. Many of us today would prefer his blot samples beyond any question, for the absence of a strong spontaneous flavor in those works adjudged as final is disappointing. Blots, Cozens instructed, were to be made endlessly and constantly. Accumulated, they represented a collection of shapes and forms, any of which could be traced and composed into an underlying composition for a painting. A blot produced on one day could be combined with other suggestions coming at other times. But this

contrivance of tracing failed to transfer the free motions and directness of the blots. Hard outlining, intact to the end, immobilizes
forms so rigidly that in most of his works Cozens seems to be denying
the license he had already come to know. Happily, however, some
of that spirit is projected to a degree sufficient to redeem his work,
which marks the entrance of spontaneous quality as a dimension of
watercolor method.

Going much further than Cozens, Turner also supported the cause
of accidental approaches as willful practice. He, it is reported, had
three young children daub his panel as only children can. At the
propitious moment he stopped them, finishing the painting a few
strokes later. With such prodigious regard for accepting chance,
Turner is credited with an overwhelming 19,400 watercolor paintings. This kind of spirit of inquiry and observation could be cultivated
more deeply by most of us.

EXPLORATION AND EXPERIMENTATION

The quality of one's ideas and his ability to present them graphically
are openly revealed in every work. The levels of accomplishment
one has attained, however, are not always satisfying and a wish to
achieve more telling results seems to be ever-present. Stronger
identifications with subject matter and improved management of
the medium usually are concluded to be the first needs. With an
open mind, serious effort to find significant means toward worthwhile ends provides a new base for action.

Assuming an exploratory attitude and outlook is not easy, for
much of our conditioning leaves little allowance for individual
judgment and expressive decisions. Often, quite unintentionally, we
actually entertain stilted expectations of a painting's content and
appearance. As a result, there seems to be a tendency to depend
almost entirely upon the more prescriptive kinds of instruction. Per-
fection without error and "never-fail" procedures may foster a mechanical proficiency, but not without encountering mannerisms,
technical imitation, and other painterly superficialities. Thus creative
energy can be lost.

Courtesy Kraushaar Galleries, New York

Artist: *JOHN HELIKER*
Title: *Collage #1*
Medium: Watercolor collage

Combined techniques sometimes resist classification. Here bits of paper, water color washes, and smudgings and lines from dry-tipped tools are intermingled. Paintings such as this created considerable confusion and controversy when submitted for showings in the water color category.

To explore a medium does not mean that its processes must be invented all over again, for the result of this would be a rather senseless duplication. Every medium retains its primary characteristics which predetermine some basic methods of handling. A grasp of conditions which promote certain effects leads to a new speculation and, if not invention, at least innovative treatment. Other options, other actions, and other materials can become eligible. Mixed media variations could not have originated or matured to legitimacy without having been justified through demonstration.

Novelty of effect and execution is to be anticipated as a part of coming to grips with a medium. Novelty, however, should not be confused with uniqueness; the former is a physical quantity, which too often is overworked and deprived of connotations. The latter is expressive. It articulates. Novelty should be prevented from taking over expressive objectives, and by the same token no medium should be forced into exhibiting entirely freakish manifestations. No effect should be admitted into a painting unless it is consistent in character with the content and the spirit of its interpretation.

The whole matter of exploration or experiment consists of observation, evaluation, and application. In watercolor painting, water, pigment, and support are each active components. Not only do they depend on one another, but each influences the other. The role of gum and pigment dispersal, the action of water, and the unusual participation of paper supports throughout the painting processes are necessarily to be understood. This interrelationship must be discovered and nurtured by the learner. Whatever one's inclination in painting may prove to become, whether visually or non-visually oriented, means and imagery are certain to be enriched through a realization of watercolor's versatility. One is wise to attempt exercises which induce a free rising of possibilities and which excite an anticipation for organizing form and context. The ultimate objective of experimentation is to stimulate a fuller comprehension of the relationships between material and expressive content, and to realize the flexible bond between the two. It prepares the individual to take command and to integrate his perceptual, intellectual, emotional, and esthetic growth.

EXERCISES

The exploration of a medium is a combination of objective observations, yet it also seeks to promote subjective relationships. The conversion of the usual into the extraordinary depends in great part upon the entry of subjective values: thinking and feeling, temper and perceptions.

Some sort of organized approach to getting acquainted with equipment and fundamental procedures is undoubtedly profitable. Elements of the unintelligible and the unintended also participate, so that control over circumstances cannot be so complete that production is absolutely depersonalized. Natural inclinations should be fostered as they emerge if individualized work habits are to develop. The handling of the brush, pen, or other tools can be overly conscious and inhibited. A little assertion of confidence, however, produces relaxed and articulating control. The artist's "handwriting," as it is called, comes into its own. New confidence in expression, richer interpretations, and greater technical versatility are the ultimate goals.

The finding of a personal style is also a prize of exploration. Influenced by our heritage, by our teachers, and by works which we admire, this is a time to look to oneself and to realize personal capability. The sample exercises included here are extemporaneous. They follow no order. There is no sequence other than that which happened from one moment to another. The problems were not all established beforehand but were precipitated as a result of prevailing circumstances. The plan was to explore all graphic elements within a common framework, in mutual association and interdependence. Line, color, area, shape, space, and other dimensions were incorporated within each exercise. Composition simply occurred, in a unity organic to the means and meanings. These exercises should provide cues for the actual paintings that are anticipated. Dealing with the whole problem should help take care of its parts.

The exercise series does not require materials of the best quality. Inexpensive papers and ink in place of more expensive paints will do for most purposes. As problems become more complex, other adjustments can be made. In this account, an odd assortment of brushes, pens, and improvised tools were worked with common 5″ x 7″ index cards. Needless to say, perhaps, all that has been said here is also meant to provide some guidelines and attitudes which might also serve the reader's investigations of each of the other media described in this book.

This example of brush, pen, and wash techniques establishes a strong movement which closes upon itself several times. It is suggestive of rock, openings, and stubble.

A random collage of newspaper bits, cloth, and ink dabbed textures, stippling, and dragged pen and twig line.

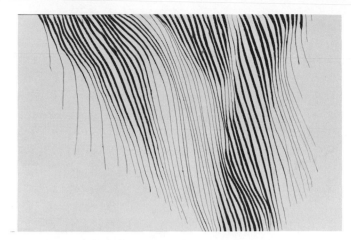

A trial in which a line is repeated side by side a number of times, with gradation changes resulting from variations in pressure.

One continuous line crossing over itself randomly, until it loses identity and becomes a mass. With change in direction, the line was made to alternate between thin then thick segments, imparting a calligraphic and geometric quality. The structural result is much like the silhouette of some forms of welded sculpture.

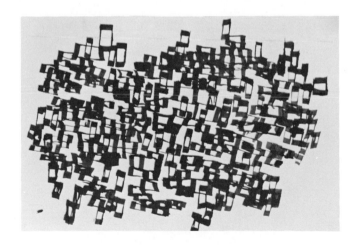

The gripping of the brush is of interest in this example. The brush, held at the handle flat against the palms of both hands, was twirled into motion by rubbing the palms back and forth against each other, like trying to start a fire with a stick. The light, indistinct spots are droppings of rubber cement.

A piece of cardboard cut into a three-pointed tool produced a paralleling system of criss-crossing lines. Spreading the hairs of a large brush between the fingers or holding more than one brush at a time can produce similar effect.

Facial tissue dipped into ink was dabbed against the paper until the ink was depleted. The effect proceeded from wet to dry as the ink dissipated.

A simple touch of the brush, begun with a definite pressure and then released with a flick, was repeated a number of times in a free pattern moving across the area of the page.

Smeared darks act as references for quick activity of pen line around them, from them, and penetrating them. The build-up begins to verge upon a release of form.

With a part of the ground wet and the remaining space moist, the stopper tip of an ink bottle is scrawled with rapid and free motion across the ground.

Dipped into a solution of ink along one edge, a tongue-depressor is dragged to form bands of area varying in width. The widths of the spaces between have also been gauged. This is a play between so-called positive and negative spaces.

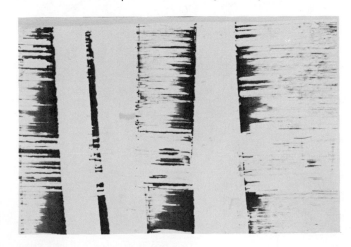

Three simple single-stroke brush marks are put into an interplay with one another while the shape of remaining space is considered simultaneously.

Single-stroke touches of the brush have been directed into several paths. While traveling in one direction, each stroke was pushed back on itself slightly, resulting in overlapping bellies.

An accumulation of heavy strokes and another of fine strokes, both following the same order of pattern, provide each other with counterpoint.

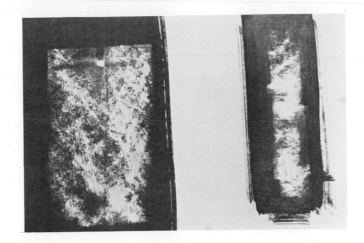

Two rectangular shapes are painted over a wax resist. Again spacing of positive and negative areas plays a part in this sample.

This free play of washes in three values and line variations emphasizes differences in length and quantity.

In this illustration darks were introduced with a pen into wide brush single-stroke washes. The dark depositings diffused as the white areas remained dry.

A collage made from remnants of torn and cut practice exercises.

This exercise was approached as a thumbnail sketch in preparation for a painting. Although loosely indicated, the composition is controlled and perhaps too final. In some ways the medium could have been given more of a chance to act.

Wet paper and ink squigglings. These are easy and commonplace. Like the tail wagging the dog, content is sometimes forced into a set of conditions. Here we are only too certain to discover polywogs or microscopic life.

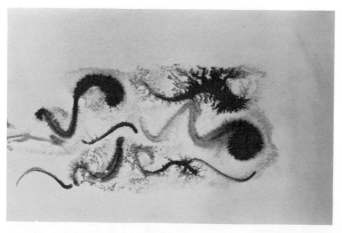

An inked paste stick has been dragged, pulled, slid laterally, and used like a blunt pen in this strata-like sample.

One wide brush crossing a page in a zig-zagging path.

A collage of two large shapes taken from other exercises. Smaller indications were made with a scrap of paper used as a brush.

41

A piece of galvanized steel was inked and pressed to the paper, with this result.

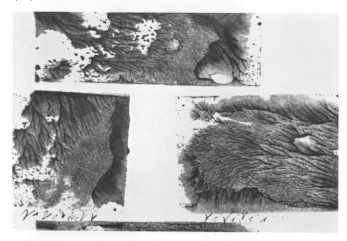

The darkest linear system was struck by discharging ink heavily from a loaded stopper. The corner of a folded piece of paper was used to pull out a second system of line from the earlier one, which still carried wet ink. Clear water brushed into fresh ink resulted in spreading washes, and a short time later diluted ink washes and touches from the tip of the brush were distributed through remaining areas.

Hog's hair bristle brush passed over itself a few times.

CHAPTER 2

Opaque Painting

Opaque painting has existed throughout recorded history. Appearing in early Egyptian wall paintings and during the days of classical Greece, it also occurs in the painting traditions of China, Japan, and India. Modern interest in technical knowledge of opaque painting, however, stems from the practices of the medieval and Renaissance periods which are the bases of the European tradition. Both transparent watercolor and oil painting methods take their origin from tempera, a painting technique using egg combinations. One other general distinction, in addition to differences in binding agents and covering power, may be made between transparent and opaque watercolor processes: the ground for tempera is not limited to paper supports. This will be explained as part of a more detailed discussion of the opaque methods.

GOUACHE

Gouache is nothing more than a physical mixture of transparent watercolors with a water soluble white pigment. Chinese white (zinc white) is the usual choice. The addition of white serves to displace the transparent character of watercolor by providing opaque body and covering power, so that dependence upon the support to provide whiteness for tonal changes becomes no longer necessary. Since gouache mixes have the ability to obscure the ground, the use of tinted papers and supports other than paper has become associated with the method. Gouache, as the name may imply, is also known as the "French method."

gouache pigments

Pigments may be directly mixed on the palette or they may be bought in ready-made mixtures. The better grades are authentic watercolor and zinc white mixes. Of far inferior quality are preparations in the category of poster colors, such as the so-called tempera paints so popular in public schools.

Like watercolors, traditional gouaches remain nonresistant to water after drying. With the introduction of rubber-based and acrylic household paints, some painters have mixed these with water colors, seemingly to good advantage. Their rapid, water impervious drying characteristics overcome the chronic difficulties of standard gouache, especially when painting over underlayers. This hybrid concoction also resists soiling, including that caused by body moistures when the painted surface is touched. Ordinarily regular gouache is easily marred in this way, to such an extent that it is wise to keep a clean piece of paper between the hands and the painting at all times.

gouache grounds

Supports for gouaches may be paper, cardboard, wood and composition board panels, or cloth. In all cases, the panel is sized with glue, usually hide, to seal and dress the surface. Care should be taken to assure that the surface of the material selected is free of

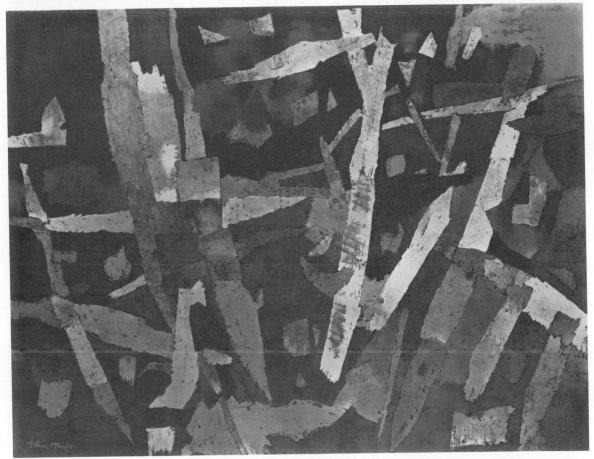

Artist: *JOHN TAYLOR*
Title: *Sanctuary, Variation #1*
Medium: Gouache

The opaque quality of gouache is readily apparent in this painting. Here the medium is employed with abstract license and regard for design and composition.

Artist: *WILLIAM KIENBUSCH*
Title: *Wave, Ocean Point*
Medium: Gouache

Rocks and waves have been romanticized into deadly stereotyped compositions. An exception to the usual is always welcome, as in this powerful interpretation of a wave. It is sound, fury, and force smashing and splitting into spray.

oil or grease. Salvaged materials are most likely to be dirty, but careless storing and handling of panel stock in the studio may also result in the soiling of painting surfaces.

When a panel is sized, the color of the panel will be that of the material used, owing to the transparency of the glue. Pigment may be added to a second sizing coat to produce other surface hues, but when a colored paper is used, of course, this will not be necessary. Bear in mind that the permanence of paper toning colors is questionable; in fact, some painters use good quality casein wall paints for toning papers instead, although expert conservationists do not recommend this alternative.

gouache practices

Interest in gouache as a pure painting medium is not of too much concern to its practitioners; instructions for its manipulation have little relationship to its separate potentialities. Too often gouache is recommended as an inexpensive substitute for oil paints, and it is perverted accordingly. The idea that gouache and oil paint are interchangeable is quite difficult to understand for, other than the covering power possessed by each, the properties of the two are quite distinct. That one should blindly imitate the other is an unfortunate concept. The real advantage of gouache is that it is capable of both transparent and opaque effects. Gouache is one of the first standardized mixed-media methods.

Time and again gouache is called upon to salvage watercolors gone awry. Chinese white and opaque tints have been mixed more often than purists and nonpurists alike will admit, in order to regain highlightings and to "correct" badly managed washes and muddied passages where transparency was intended. Because "doctoring" is easily detectable, even when sparingly done, quite a few painters feel averse to the practice, preferring to destroy works which do not measure up to their high standards. If thickly applied, gouache paints tend to crack and chip and, it might be added, where one medium has been poorly handled, there is nothing to prevent clumsiness with the second.

Gouaches dry lighter than when freshly mixed. Overstating color intensity will help to compensate for this feature. When mixing,

Artist: *YASUO KUNIYOSHI*
Title: *Clown*
Medium: Casein

The dry and linear quality of opaque watercolor media is exercised in this poignant portrait. However, some thin washings, like veils, are also employed, after the method of glazing and scumbling in oil.

paints should be kept moist as long as possible. Special cloth covered palettes have been used to keep color active; the cloth maintains a sufficient saturation. Wetting of the support also prolongs the manipulative state of gouache mixtures. Because the amounts of water may be increased at any moment of work, the support usually is held horizontally. This permits color to "flood-on" without running and merging. When a gouache painting reaches a dry state the matching of colors is difficult, and even if it is done well, seams will show, at times necessitating the repainting of entire areas. The conditions most ideal for gouache are relatively short-lived and, consequently, gouache works are executed with a more spontaneous character and within a short time—*alla prima*, or in a single sitting. Hog bristle and single-stroke lettering brushes are highly favored by gouache exponents.

A convenient means of transition from transparent to opaque media is afforded via gouache mixtures. Often gouache bases are further tempered by the addition of egg yolk, egg emulsions, emulsified waxes, oils, and varnishes. These simple modifications of gouache are primitive forms of emulsified temperas.

THE TEMPERAS

The temperas important to easel painting are those prepared with emulsions. An emulsion is a suspension of globules of one liquid in a second liquid. Neither liquid is miscible with the other—for example, as the oil and water combined into tempera emulsions. The suspended drops do not coalesce because of the viscous or plastic film surrounding each. An emulsion may be either of two kinds: an oil suspended in water or water suspended in oil. Egg yolk is a natural example of an oil-in-water emulsion, in which minute globules of egg oil are distributed throughout a primarily watery liquid. The ratio is reversed in water-in-oil emulsions, and the dispersal of water through oily materials is much like that observed in butter. Of concern to us is the oil-in-water emulsion type.

The stability of emulsions is dependent upon the size of the globules and the adequacy of the film enveloping each to prevent their coalescing. The more minute the emulsified particle, the better will it remain in suspension. Power-driven mixers are best for agitating emulsions into the smallest particle sizes and into more uniform dispersions. To combine the ingredients of an emulsion, one is poured in a thin stream into the other while being beaten. Small quantities of emulsion may be made by vigorous manual shaking in small containers, such as calibrated 4 oz. or 8 oz. covered bottles. Though not as convenient, an ordinary egg-beater may be used.

An emulsifier, or stabilizer, is a necessary ingredient in producing emulsions. When none is naturally present, as in egg yolk, an emulsifying agent is introduced to give the interface a film producing property. Although all emulsions are also colloidal solutions, all colloids are not emulsions; egg white and casein are colloidal solutions which become emulsions when vegetable oil is shaken into the solutions. The usual emulsifying agents for oil-in-water systems are sodium and potassium oleates, which are also water soluble colloids. In the action resulting from this mixture, oil particles become surrounded by, first, a layer of oil molecules, then, over that, a layer of molecules of the emulsifying agent, and, lastly, a covering of water molecules.

When tempera emulsions dry, a hard oil film is formed. The clear character of the stabilizer and oil droplets is retained, and the two ingredients appear to form a homogeneous mass. The relatively small amount of oil in painting emulsions is sufficient to bind pigments.

casein tempera

Casein paints are among the oldest known in use. One variation, derived from skim milk and lime, has long been used for the painting of walls. As an adhesive, casein is extremely strong and lasting, but because lime casein is soluble in water and because it sets and hardens almost immediately, it is a difficult easel painting medium. Ammonia casein, prepared from casein and ammonium carbonate, is workable and reliable. Not soluble in water, ammonia casein is considerably more durable.

When casein paints harden, they form a fibrous, horn-like, and brittle surface. Like all emulsions in the albumen class, casein encourages and supports the growth of molds, but spraying with a 4 per cent solution of formaldehyde protects casein paintings from mold ravage. Formaldehyde also hardens or tans casein, increasing its resistance to water and moisture. Casein temperas prepared commercially tend to harden in their tubes; the addition of glycerine will minimize this tendency, but will also increase the solubility of the casein in water. Don't hesitate to feel for "give" in the tube when buying casein paints. Freshness is important. Be certain that screw caps are always snugly replaced.

Depending upon the oil used, casein emulsions will yellow. Linseed oil discolors most, poppy-seed somewhat less, and stand oil least of all. When buying prepared casein paints, there is no way to ascertain the stabilizer contained; however, the best quality preparations are certain to be reliable against pronounced yellowing. Upon drying, casein colors lighten in value and assume a somewhat powdery surface effect. At least one manufacturer recommends its media varnish to compromise the differences in value and to provide the surface with a glowing, wax-like patina. The media varnish is incorporated with the usual casein painting procedures as follows: First, isolate underdrawings with a layer of a mixer of white shellac (one part) and shellac thinner (2 parts). Allow to dry. Then apply a thin coat of casein media varnish to the panel, quickly wiping it away with a soft, absorbent cloth. The very light layer of varnish which remains will stay moist for several hours. Proceed with caseins and water, working directly into the varnish. To resume painting, as on the following day, repeat varnish application.

As the painting dries, the varnish is taken up by the casein, imparting a resemblance to oil painting. The use of varnish enables casein underpainting to remain better intact as painting progresses.

Artists' casein colors are widely used in the commercial art field. It has great imitative versatility, approximating appearances not only of oil painting but of other media also. A great favorite with illustrators, it combines well in mixed-media techniques and has been used even to simulate pastels.

polymer temperas

Polymer temperas are preparations made with synthetic resins prepared from a variety of unsaturated, organic materials by means of chemical polymerization. They may also be produced by a second process, by condensation from oxygen-containing compounds.

Combining both processes makes possible still other artificial resins. The polymer resins which are commonly used in the preparation of paints, lacquers, and varnishes are the acrylic resins, some of the alkyd resins, the styrene resins, and the vinyl resins.

The polymer temperas have been marketed to make a strong bid to replace all customary paint preparations. Claim is made for a perfect, all-purpose medium, which not only has none of the defects of other media but also excels on all points favoring any of them. Indeed, it can give the appearance of watercolor, of gouache, of tempera, or of oil. But if there is any question to raise, it surely must concern the emphasis upon substitution. How can one explain how a piece of work done with water as the medium, and without the benefit of oil siccatives, qualifies to be shown and accepted as an oil painting? The most remarkable thing about polymer resins is that they can be used in so many ways that conformity to traditional painting concepts can be relinquished. Painting can even get off the flat panel, so to speak, as in the sculpture-paintings of Robert Mallary.

Polymer paints may be used on virtually any surface—paper, wall, canvas, fiberglass, and wood. Collage and montage techniques are clearly implicit, if given a chance to be developed. Frankly, new esthetic and formal criteria not only are possible through the polymers but should be more actively sought.

egg tempera painting   Egg tempera painting is probably the most important of the developed painting methods; both watercolor and oil painting owe much of their being to it. For this reason, and because it is a medium distinct in itself and in its processes, a detailed account is necessary.

During the fourteenth and fifteenth centuries egg tempera was most prominent, but with the coming into its own of oil painting as we know it today, egg media went into a decline, although only for a short time. Not discontinued entirely, it managed inconspicuous survival in such places as secluded monasteries. In the early part of the nineteenth century there was a revival of interest in early Italian painting, and with it was rediscovered Cennini's treatise, *Libro dell' arte* (*Painter's Handbook*), ca. 1432/37. The descriptions of painting practices of the times as given there were transcribed and translated into various languages.

Artist: **LEO MANSO**
Title: *Tanka—The Torch*
Medium: Cloth-Paper—Sobo Adhesive

"This is a cloth-paper collage on heavy paperboard. Cloth and paper are stained with Acquatec Acrylic Polymer Emulsion. Some elements are first prepared with Acquatec Gesso and then glazed with thinned color (Acquatec medium and water). Each element is permitted to dry thoroughly before applying, thus becoming absolutely water-fast. The work is applied flat, each element being coated on the underside with Sobo adhesive, and then washed down with water to remove excess. This process, since it is organic and not coldly planned, results in several levels or layers of adhered material. The wetting process results in coating the entire work with a thin film of Sobo adhesive binding everything into a unity."—Leo Manso

Artist: *ANDREW WYETH*
Title: *Mother Archie's Church*
Medium: Tempera

With a technique close to that of the pure egg tempera method, a desolate and neglected interior is depicted, dark with shadow except for an invasion of light from the outside which throws itself across a section of cracking ceiling and envelops a white bird poised in flight —all like some omen of hope and promise.

Present egg tempera usage appears at least in part to be an off-shoot of its adaptation for mural purposes. Tudor Hart championed it in Europe among muralists in the 1920s; in the United States renewal of interest materialized in the studios of N. C. Wyeth, Thomas Hart Benton, Charles Sheeler, Ben Shahn, and others. Considerable egg tempera research was conducted at Harvard early in this century. At the present time, important exponents are Andrew Wyeth and Peter Hurd, both of whom succeed in the tradition of N. C. Wyeth. Zoltan Sepeshy and Kenneth Callahan must be credited with their inquiry and work also. In spite of the restrictive technical nature of egg tempera media, each has demonstrated by his individuality the versatility possible with the medium.

EGG TEMPERA CHARACTERISTICS

Egg tempera is a medium complete in itself. While it is a direct ancestor of both watercolor and oil media, it is neither transparent nor opaque. It depends for its effects upon layerings of semiopaque colors, one on the other. The coloration qualities for which tempera is highly regarded can be achieved if the layers are kept translucent. Each layer of paint serves as a tinted undercoat for successive layers of color, and there is no obliteration of any of them. Each is seen at the same time, mixing optically into color and value harmonies. The principle of optical mixing of colors is also employed in the rendering of light and dark gradations and in the transition of one color to another by means of short hatching strokes. The surface of egg paints is smooth and devoid of any impasto.

MANIPULATION OF EGG TEMPERA

Basically, tempera painting is a line technique which is closely akin to drawing. Tempera cannot be blended like oil or washed like watercolor because it is almost instantly absorbed by its gesso ground. Attempts to blend colors together with water in the manner of oil painting are not possible. Washes of color over a freshly painted layer do not blend as they do with watercolor. The full range of transparency to opacity, therefore, must be achieved by other means. From generalized indications to the most refined detailings, crosshatching is the key manipulation. Variations in crosshatching create color variations. The spacing between lines, their widths, their coloration, their degree of opacity, and how they affect underlayers—which also consist of hatched screenings in addition to washed-in areas—must be understood in developing rapport with tempera.

From the foregoing, egg is seen to be very low in malleability. The free use of water will improve it in that respect, but the result not only may be too much like that of watercolor, but will also not have sufficient body to be useful in the final stages of painting. As explained elsewhere, the addition of oil will retard initial drying. Therefore, to provide a flowing quality to the paints sufficient water should always be used. For this purpose either vinegar or acetic acid may be added; either will also make the yolk less greasy.

During the fifteenth century, the painting sequence began with a charcoal drawing on the gesso. Tempera paint was used to fix the drawing. The practice of dusting off excess charcoal by slapping a cloth against the drawing is helpful in avoiding smudging when brushing on the medium. Occasionally the drawing was developed with India ink or monochrome washes, instead of in outline, to give effects of light and shadow. Similar practice, it will be remembered, was employed in conjunction with the four English watercoloring methods above (pp. 12-17).

After the outline was fixed, an underpainting consisting of washes of paint flowed on with squirrel-hair brushes was introduced to establish local colors. Areas where flesh tones and shadows were to be painted were underpainted in terre verte (green earth) so as to establish body-part form or structure. Other detailings, such as draperies, were painted in a fairly direct manner with three distinct tones of light, middle, and dark color. Hair was similarly done. To facial and other skin areas not in shadow, a thinned out or tinted flesh color was applied, and over the lips and cheeks a pink color.

In the final phase of painting, details such as hair and draperies were finished by the addition of highlights and dark accents. Allowing the green underpainting to show through in the shadowed areas, light, medium, and dark pinks were also used at this point for the modeling of flesh. This treatment is notable for the opalescent effect which results. The shadows in faces and hands were deepened more with a greenish-brown mixture. Black was used to define details and white to mark highlights.

Technical departures from classic procedures are always bound to occur. The combination of oil with watercolors appears to have been practiced early by masters of the Venetian school. This consisted of tempera underpainting over which oil colors were painted. The method was regarded as secret and its communication was under

Artist: *BEN SHAHN*
Title: *Ave*
Medium: Tempera

The temperas of Ben Shahn employ a flatter, posteresque handling, while expressing a curious mixture of intimacy, anonymity, and loneliness as part of commonplace happenings.

penal restriction. This technique seems to have fallen short of the artists' expectation, however, and was discontinued. Similar treatment is associated with John of Bruges, the supposed inventor of oil painting, and with John Van Eyck, whom Vasari credits with the invention of painting in oil.

When either full color range tempera or monotone underpainting is to be used, it and the absorbent ground must be isolated from the overpainting. Retouch varnish, shellac in five parts of alcohol, or gelatine solution may be brushed on with a large brush. The dry

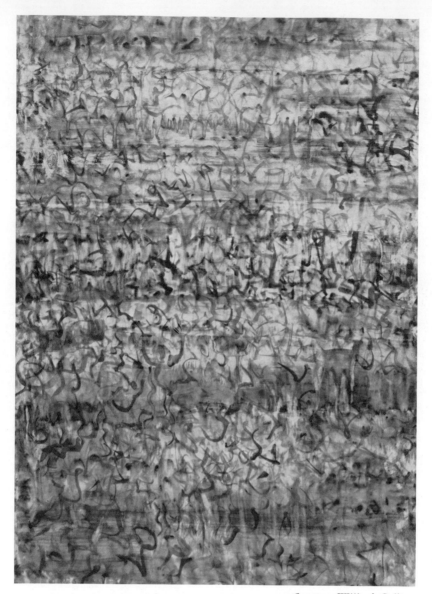

Artist: MARK TOBEY
Title: *Time of Tides*
Medium: Tempera

Soft and elusive, muted, almost intangible, this artist's personalized and intertwining calligraphy of light and dark line suggests forms momentarily, as when sea touches sand, rippling, foaming, then sinking into nothingness.

tempera painting will be protected and the oil paint will not be absorbed, thus limiting brushwork. The fast drying of the tempera underpainting hastens the completion of paintings which are to be finished with oil glazings.

A mixed media process used by Roger van der Weyden and other artists of the German and Flemish schools of the fifteenth and sixteenth centuries is known today as the "wet-in-wet technique," an interchangeable combination of egg tempera and oil medium. Some claim that this technique provided the transition from egg tempera to oil painting.

True egg tempera painting is a slow process, often requiring months to complete a single painting. It is a technique which allows for precise linear draughtsmanship and lends itself to decorative effects. The difficulty of making changes as work progresses and the impossibility of working colors on the support itself are the limitations within which techniques must be developed.

Much of the preparation for egg tempera is done by the artist or the student in the studio. Because prepared egg temperas and gesso panels are not readily available, home manufacture is a necessity. As an aid, it is hoped that the comments and information which follow will be adequate.

BRUSHES

Extra attention should be given to the selection of brushes for egg tempera painting. Hair, shape, size, and quantity are relevant to successful control of the medium. Visual characteristics and the mechanics of producing them are dependent upon appropriate brush choice. The size of the painting and of the areas to be worked at a given time are also determining factors.

Sable brushes are the only satisfactory tools for tempera purposes. In spite of the initial expense, in the end they can be the most economical. Camel's hair tufts are difficult to keep in shape and to manipulate without unruly behavior because of their softness. Oriental brushes are useful with thinned color mixings only. The usual hairs, such as fiber, sheep, and other domestic animals, are not limber enough to match the spring and deft certainty of sable hairs. Of the two kinds of sable, the red is far superior in every way to the black,

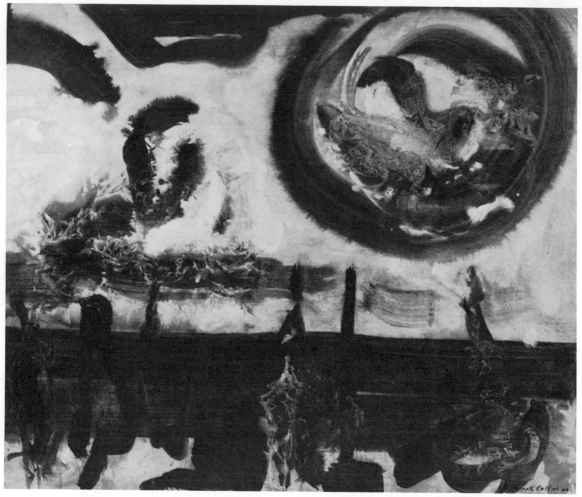

Artist: *KENNETH CALLAHAN*
Title: *Patterns #1 1962*
Medium: Tempera

    In contrast to traditional egg tempera examples, here the ground is rice paper and the medium is egg with equal part stand oil. The approach is direct and broad-brushed, and the absorbency of the paper is allowed to participate. Water combines with oil to produce distinct effects, and at least one more effect is achieved by dabbing at the fresh surface with crumpled paper, lifting pigment and leaving an imprint of creases.

and any difference in price between the two is not appreciable enough to warrant a selection of the black over red.

Although one good brush of high quality and of small size and good point could be made to manage the execution of a tempera painting from start to finish, for good reasons the use of considerably more than one brush is advisable. As many as twenty or thirty brushes, at least, are usual rather than the exception. Many painters like to use a fresh brush for every mixture, to preserve the tone of each. Such practice also minimizes the necessity of frequent interruption to wash out brushes. Over a period of time, a fistful of brushes in use together will outlast the same number and more which are used alone or in small lots. When a big supply is maintained, by adding and replacing when necessary, each brush will wear down more slowly and evenly, thereby prolonging its life.

The quality and quantity of sables are not necessarily beyond the average painter's means. Large brushes are not necessary; at best they allow the laying down of thicker mixings of tempera. Nor do large brushes serve to hasten the painting tempo and the coverage of area. Confidently maneuvered, any good small sable can accomplish the same ends as speedily. Smaller brushes, then, not only produce a savings in cost but also offer more facility.

Another economy may be realized if sign-painters' brushes are substituted for sable watercolor brushes. In watercolor brushes the hairs are mounted in metal ferrules and the handles are finished in varnish or enameled. The sign painter's brush is of less expensive materials and ornateness, but they are available in red sable the equal of any and at quite reasonable prices. They differ in the use of quill mountings, with swan quill the largest, goose next, and crow the smallest.

The most adaptable of brush shapes to tempera is the round tip. This is true of sable brushes and, under certain circumstances, of bristle. Round brushes carry more color than do flat brushes of comparable size. They also produce a more even stroke.

Bristle brushes, when they are used, should be of the best grade available. The hair length should be much longer than that usually associated with bristle varieties—as much as two inches, and probably more. Such a brush should be densely fashioned and springy.

Most often used to block-in under layers and broad areas, they also serve well in larger paintings by providing strokes in better proportion to the dimensions of the panel.

Loading the brush   Traditional tempera manipulation is done with a brush pressed almost dry. In fact, the qualities to be gained are frequently compared to those resulting of building-up techniques with pencil, with emphasis upon quick and easy strokes. To maintain even tone and other consistent regularities of stroke, proper loading of the brush is essential. For uniform strokes, dip the brush into the prepared color, stir it thoroughly, then remove excess paint from the brush by first wiping it all around against the lip of the container and then across a clean cloth or the back of the hand. Color combinations mixed on the palette are lifted into the brush in as much the same manner as possible.

Basic brush positions   The tip of the brush and its heel are used to accomplish distinct purposes. For the drawing of lines the point is used. Changes in pressure are also applied according to variations desired. For "filling" areas and for blunted strokes the heel is pressed against the panel.

TEMPERA SUPPORTS

Any and all of the temperas may be applied to any surface which is absorbent to greater or less degree. Paper, paper boards, canvas, and wood are typical materials. Priming coats are not required with any of these, since the first underlayer will absorb sufficiently to serve for the ground.

Various ways of working with tempera will frequently decide the need for other ways of priming. If there must be an absorbent ground primers made with oil or other film forming ingredients, such as rubber and vinyl, are not appropriate. White pigment tempered with egg yolk is simple and reliable and eliminates the need of preparing water grounds which require far more complicated instructions. Zinc white or titanium white mixed with yolk of egg and water provides a covering which dries so quickly that hardly any time need be allowed before application of each required coat.

Hardening quickly, panels made in this way are ready for painting almost immediately.

Before discussing sizing and priming, some comments should be made about the construction of panels. Tempered masonite, ⅛″ thick, may be used for paintings of any size, provided that it is reinforced, or cradled, whenever the side exceeds three feet. Thicker masonite may be used instead, or, for very large works, other kinds of building boards as thick as ½″ may be chosen. This often can mean contending with a problem of weight. The thinnest masonite, cradled, is as rigid as the thickest of boards and far less heavy.

A cradle is nothing more than an open wood frame, mitered or dovetailed at the corners, and—depending upon the size of the panel —with evenly spaced and interlocked horizontal and vertical crosspieces; it is actually a lattice. Redwood which is light, sturdy, and resistant to warping, is excellent for the purpose. A suitable size is 1″ x 2″ stock. In constructing the cradle, plan for each piece to be placed on edge against the back of the panel. Use any good glue, such as hide, casein, or the newer epoxies. Clamp or place the panel and cradle under weight until the glue sets. Do not nail or screw them together through the face of the panel. If not used as a painting support, this type of panel is very serviceable for stretching papers.

Some masonite is smooth on both sides and others are smooth on one side only. The smooth side is best for priming, but the "rough" side seldom is primed as its regular and deep mechanical texture is almost impossible to fill in. Hesitantly, for fear that the observation be interpreted as a recommendation, some gentle people liken the texture to that of canvas. There the similarity is better forgotten.

For better adhering of sizing and ground coats, the smooth side is roughened somewhat with any coarse abrasive, such as rough sanding papers or a rasp. The full surface is scraped with a scouring action, leaving networks of scratches over scratches. A hide glue sizing is applied to this side as well as to the back and sides of the panel and, if provided, the cradling also. Glue priming is capable of deforming even the thickest of panels in drying. The panel's back may be sealed further with a good waterproof paint. If cardboard is primed with glue, it should be put under pressure, flat, when the glue passes its tacky stage. Warped cardboard is extremely difficult to straighten.

GESSO

Most widely accepted as the ground for egg tempera methods is gesso. A glue primer, it is a combination of either glue or gelatine, chalk, and a little bit of white pigment. Titanium white is preferred for its greater ability to reflect light. Since there are fairly numerous variations, perhaps it is best to follow the instructions provided with standardized commercial gesso and glues to prepare gesso-type grounds. A requirement for a workable gesso is that it be neither too absorbent nor too nonabsorbent. If a glue solution is too dilute, a ground of a weak and soft density results. A typically fine lined crackle may be expected later for the same reason. Too great a concentration of glue produces a ground which is hard and non-absorbent. It will withstand cracking.

The glue solution to be combined with the whiting (chalk) can be easily tested for its strength while it is being heated. A small amount of the warmed glue is mixed with some whiting and brushed onto a piece of wood or masonite—whichever will be used for the panels themselves. After a short wait for the sample to dry, it is rubbed with sandpaper, No. 2/0. Rapid cutting of the gesso and filling of the sandpaper signify a too soft ground and a too dilute glue mixture just as resistance to sanding denotes too much glue stuff. When too dilute, more pieces of soaked glue should be added to the glue solution; concentrated mixtures can be adjusted by diluting with hot water.

No matter what primer is chosen, its application must result in a series of smooth and even coatings, each free of irregularities, impurities, and "pinholes." If the primer solution is kept thin—somewhat like milk—and if each coat but the last is allowed at least three hours to dry, a good ground with strong reflecting quality can be expected. The final coat is applied while the last previous coat is still in a damp stage. A soft, wide brush, at least three inches wide, such as a varnish brush, is useful for laying down the ground, except the first coat. The hake, with which rice papers are stretched, also will serve this purpose excellently. Stiff brushes and too thick gesso mixtures account for high-ridged brush streaks and ragged brush overlaps which are extremely difficult to eliminate without introducing other kinds of surface difficulties.

When a circular rubbing down with a soft pad of evenly dampened cotton cloth is attempted, several changes can take place. Rubbing too long in one spot will remove the ground in that area. And wherever ridges are successfully removed the gesso becomes much harder and less absorbent than the rest of the panel. Later, when the panel is polished by sandings, greater resistance to sandpapers will be noticed.

The last stage in the preparation of the gesso is its polishing. Prior to painting upon it, the ground is buffed to a smooth finish, like burnished ivory. For reasons of effect, as in the case of water-color paper, the surface need not be absolutely smooth, however. A coarse tooth will impart a dry quality, and a semifine finish lends well to heavier and generalized crosshatched effects. More refined detailings and hatchings need correspondingly smoother grounds. While smooth finishes are usual, certain artificial textures are imposed in many instances. Pumice or silicon may be added to the gesso for the final coat. Or the last coat may be stippled, sprayed, or spattered during application. Rough cloths, such as toweling and homespun, may be pressed to the surface while it is fresh. The ground may also be pressed with the palm of the hand while it is half dry. Tapping against the surface all over with the blunt end of a stencil knife will provide a rough surface of softened indentations. Rough or smooth, all surface treatments are polished in the same way.

For the final dressing of the ground, it is rubbed down with fine sandpapers, of which No. 4/0 garnet paper is perhaps most satisfactory. If an even smoother and harder final surface is desired, No. 6/0 garnet paper or the fine steel wool, No. 00, can be used. Induced textures will not be lost during the process. All glue grounds should be wiped off with a dampened cloth before being painted upon.

Wall paints made with casein have been used in place of traditional gesso, but their use is not advised. Actually, casein has been replaced extensively by other binding ingredients, principally those in the polymer class, but because they are not absorbent, polymers definitely cannot be used for egg tempera grounds.

Applying gesso   One of the surest ways of applying gesso to a panel is to cover small squares of area at a time. The method simply consists of covering a small area at a time with brush strokes applied in motions from left to right, followed by straking-off strokes from top to bottom. When the panel is covered, the second coat is begun almost at once. The proper time for the application of a following coating is when a dull cast in the previous coat replaces the shine indicative of wetness.

With the second coat the order of the direction of stroke and strake are reversed in relation to the first coat. Strokes run from top to bottom and straking-off runs from left to right. The first square of the second coat is made half the size of the squares of the first coat so that the edges of the squares making up each layer will not coincide in position. More even gesso accumulation is the result. The third coat is a repetition of the first and the fourth is a repetition of the second. Five coats are sufficient, but if more are required the order of application should be obvious.

A stippling method may be employed in place of brushing methods or in combination with them. The difference between them consists in the manner of depositing gesso and the body and surface character of the gesso layers. In one instance gesso is brushed on, in the other it is tapped on by means of striking the loaded brush on its side against the panel. The lifting of the brush produces a soft even stipple, which will be found to be advantageous over the irregular and ridged strokes resulting from brushing when the surface of the gesso is scraped or sanded evenly later. Because the brush is tapped to the panel, the layers are called *tap coats*.

Some points to remember when building up tap coats are:

1. Keep the brush (a large round one) fully loaded at all times.
2. Avoid back and forth or up and down motions. When slapped against the panel, the brush should be pushed forward only, away and never toward oneself.
3. When combined in alternating layers, tap coats are laid over brush coats.

Finishing gesso surfaces   Sanding gesso is one way of giving the surface a smooth and even finish. The process is slow and not acceptable to everyone; some practitioners prefer to scrape the surface while others advocate grinding the surface down with fine abrasives or whetstones. And of course, combinations of these methods are both possible and practical. Smoothing of gesso should not be attempted until the panel has been permitted to dry completely. At least two days should be allowed.

The blade of a plane serves well as a scraper. A blade may be made, if necessary, from a strip of thin metal, preferably steel because of its hardness and its ability to stay sharpened. If a scraper is devised, a width of two or three inches is adequate. The cutting edge should be perfectly straight and sharply tapered on one side, like the edge of a chisel. Given a slight burr along the edge, the scraper will cut rapidly and evenly. To put a burr on the edge, steady the blade vertically on a flat sharpening stone (Arkansas), and drag it firmly across the stone, leading in the direction of the blade edge. The burr serrates the edge just sufficiently to wear down the gesso with a crisscrossing of very fine, shallow furrows. Round off the ends of the cutting edge.

Before scraping is begun, some way of gauging the depth of any uneven places and of localizing the areas to be scraped is necessary. If the surface is covered with charcoal dust, a gray tone will remain when it is wiped. During the course of scraping, the gesso is gradually removed until the panel is completely white again. White will appear first where gesso has been deposited high, and last at the lowest level. It is quite possible to overscrape sections, even to the extent of baring the panel. Moderate pressure, short and regular cutting strokes, and a systematic procedure are reliable manual controls. Least difficulty is encountered when each stroke overlaps another, in a crisscross arrangement on a common axis, very much like a herringbone series in principle. Several light scrapings of the panel are more likely to assure desired results than one heavy-handed assault.

Proper grip of the scraper is important. Held in both hands, with the thumbs pressing at the middle of one side, the scraper is pulled toward oneself. The blade should be kept vertical to the plane of the panel and the thumbs should be against the side on which the edge is burred, facing the operator, and in the direction of scraping. The ground edge should be on the backside. Actually, the correct position for the scraper can be easily found through practice trial. The difference in ease of cutting is unmistakable.

Grinding   A small whetstone, some water, and a sponge can provide a highly satisfactory surface finish. Working a small area at a time, the gesso is wetted with cold water and rubbed with a whetstone which has been dipped in water. A rotary motion is employed, and the resulting paste of softened gesso is lifted with a sponge (a cloth may be used instead). One should be careful to avoid the entry of large grains of grit under the stone, which can cause irreparable marring.

Removing gesso   When defects in a panel are many, because of improper proportioning of ingredients, poor application, and the presence of pinholes and foreign materials, the panel may be salvaged and a new start made. To remove gesso coatings entirely and conveniently, cover the surface with wet sawdust and let it stand overnight. A spatula will then move easily through the softened layers and clear the panel in the shortest time.

Pinholes   The most serious defect of gesso grounds is the "pinhole." A pinhole is a minute hole in the surface which is caused by air bubbles occurring during the application of the first gesso layer. To prevent pinholes, the closest attention to the mixing, heating, and application of gesso should be maintained. It is believed that dust, cold and damp atmospheric conditions, and high surface tension in the mixture bear relationship to this fault. Both too dilute and too concentrated glue solutions also account for pinholes. Too brisk stirring of hot glue gesso encourages formation of air bubbles in the mixture. To forestall pinholes, the first coat should be applied with a stiff brush, or it may be smeared on by hand, but in either case, forcefully and with a uniform spreading. If pinholes have not been averted with the first coat, the addition of oxgall to following coats often eliminates them. Each coat is brushed on in the direction opposite to that of the preceding one, alternating at right angles to one another.

The making of gesso panels is a long and exacting task. Constant attention to the coordinating of procedures is necessary, and it is best to prepare several panels at the same time.

EGG EMULSION MEDIA

Some recipes call for only the yolk of the egg, while other emulsions, to which oils, varnishes, or both are added, usually use the whole egg. The same ingredients, differing only in proportion, are used whether whole egg or yolk only is employed.

Fresh eggs are best, of course; the fresher the egg, the longer its working period will be. White-shelled eggs are considered superior to others, more out of tradition than fact.

The separating of white from yolk is a relatively simple but exacting process, just like that employed in the kitchen. This consists of cracking a raw egg into two halves and pouring the yolk and white back and forth until the white is drained and only the yolk remains, still in its sac. At this point the yolk may be put into a cup, punctured, and stirred with one or two tablespoons of water. A certain amount of white clinging to the membrane will enter into the mix, but it may be lessened by straining the yolk through muslin either before or after thinning with water. Another method, again not the best but certainly convenient, is to break the egg into a strainer, allowing the white to sieve itself through and afterward draining the yolk in like fashion into a cup or other appropriate container. The most complete means of separating the yolk requires a little more careful operation and handling of the yolk. After the white has been poured off, gently transfer the yolk into the palm of one hand, then roll it to the other palm. Do this several times, wiping the releasing hand with each exchange. The sac is "wiped dry" by depositing the white on the hands. Gently held by the thumb and forefinger, the yolk is very carefully lifted from its rest on one palm and suspended over a container. With a sharp point, such as a knife or pin, rupture the membrane. When the amount of yolk desired has been reached, add distilled water, thinning the yolk considerably.

SEPARATING PURE YOLK FROM EGG

1. A fresh egg is cracked against a jar. Close at hand is paper toweling, which will be needed very soon afterward for wiping hands.

2. White is drained, half shell at a time, while passing the yolk from half to half.

3. Having drained all of the white except for that which still coats the yolk's membrane, the yolk is transferred to the palm of one hand.

4.   The yolk is passed from palm to palm several times, and some of the white comes away from the sac.

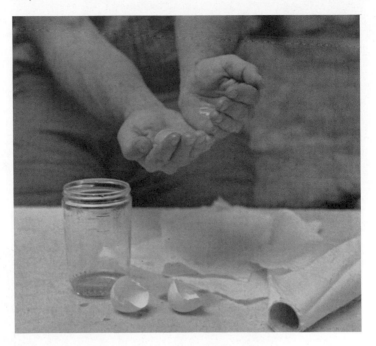

5.   Holding the yolk in one hand, the other hand wipes itself by crumpling a paper towel. It is a good idea to tear toweling into convenient sizes in advance.

6.   The yolk is passed to the other hand, and the wiping of white from the other hand is repeated as before.

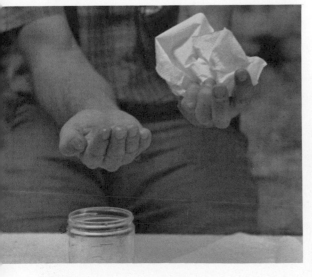

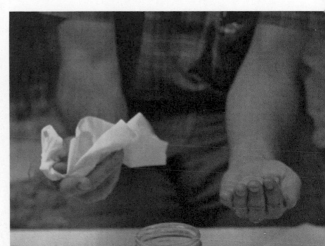

7. The knot of the yolk's sac is lifted. It is by this umbilical-like cord that the sac will be held prior to releasing of the yolk.

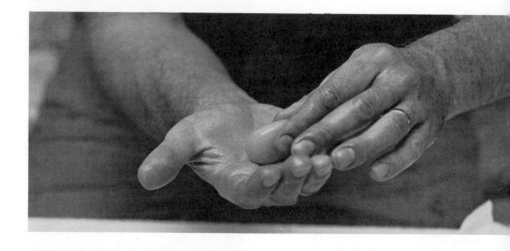

8. The yolk is carefully gripped between the thumb and forefinger.

9. Positioned over a container, the sac is ruptured with a pin and drained of yolk.

The whites may be used as a binder. Called *glair*, it was once combined into color for the illumination of manuscripts.

The addition of preservatives in egg emulsions really is not necessary, as refrigeration is more effective. If kept in a cool and dark place, egg preparations will not begin to spoil for four days. If the egg mixture is to be kept for a more indeterminate time, two or three drops of vinegar or three per cent acetic acid will not only act as a preservative but will also reduce the greasiness of the medium. Boric acid, salicylic acid, and carbolic acid have also been used as additives, but, as a word of caution, remember that acids react with whiting and other chalks, cadmiums, and ultramarine. A drop of oil of cloves or small amounts of alcohol are better preservatives under the circumstances.

Emulsion variations The simplest egg emulsions are the whole egg, its white, or its yolk. Other egg emulsions are egg in any of those forms combined with oils or varnishes. These alterations determine differences in manipulation and body. Fat tempera mediums provide heavier impasto qualities, which, suggestive of oil techniques, support effects in that direction. Lean emulsions, those made without oil, are closer in body to water color. The more complex an emulsion is, the more difficult it is to prepare and the more subject it is to the separation of its ingredients—mainly of the oil. For this reason only the simpler and proved emulsions are regarded as reliable. One apparent advantage of emulsions of egg over egg alone is resistance to spoilage when in use.

Some classic recipes Some tempera recipes have been passed along from artist to artist and from place to place, while others have been discovered through inquiry into early writings and through laboratory analysis. Of these the more favored and simplest to prepare are described here.

EGG AND OIL VARIATIONS

    a.   1 part whole egg
        1 part stand oil

> b. 1 part egg yolk
> *1 part stand oil*
>
> c. (Father Paulinus' Recipe)
> *4 whole eggs*
> *1 tbs. boiled linseed oil*
> *1 tsp. vinegar*

Thoroughly shake together the eggs and whites. Combine the oil and vinegar, adding it to the egg and again shaking well. Passed through muslin, or cheesecloth, the emulsion is stored in any bottle with a tight-fitting cover.

> d. 1 whole egg
> *stand oil, 1/4 to 1/3 the volume of the egg*
> *oil of cloves, 3 to 5 drops*
> *distilled water, two to three times the volume of egg and oil*

Stir the egg completely—with a fork in a shallow bowl is fine. Add the oil, then the essence of cloves, stirring vigorously with each addition. Combine with distilled water, again stirring thoroughly, and strain through cloth.

EGG AND VARNISH VARIATIONS

> a. 1 egg yolk
> *distilled water, equal to or less than volume of egg*
> *copal varnish, 3 to 5 drops*
> *vinegar, enough to emulsify varnish*

To emulsify the varnish, stir it with a few drops of vinegar. Add to the thoroughly shaken combination of egg and water. The emulsification is complete when there is no sign of varnish after much shaking and after standing awhile.

> b. 1 whole egg
> *damar (or copal) varnish, 1/2 to 1/3 the volume of egg*
> *oil of cloves, 3 to 5 drops*
> *distilled water, two to three times the combined volume of*
> *other ingredients*

Follow instructions as for d. in egg/oil emulsion listing.

Egg yolk   Pure yolk is usually thinned with water, in amounts which suit individual preferences and according to the effects to be secured. While cutting down the greasiness of yolk by itself, thinner mixtures assure fuller loadings of the brush with colors, easier manipulation, quicker coverage of area, and a faster drying rate. Tempered color itself is quite thick, and it too should be diluted with water. If thinned well, the mixture is more likely to be deposited evenly while enabling rapid and smooth brush motions. When in contact with the ground, the brush should not feel hampered in its actions, as though needing to be pushed and pulled to complete its passages and release the pigment. Thick mixes dry slowly enough to hinder painting progress and to introduce serious difficulties of technique. Unless color layers dry quickly, building-up is not possible without disturbing and destroying those areas of underlayer which have not hardened sufficiently.

The addition of chemical preservatives to egg mixtures does not prevent an egg mixture from forming a hard crust on the sides and lips of its container while painting is in progress. Spoilage of the mixture is hastened unless this condition is nullified. One useful countermeasure is to transfer and seal unused emulsion in a clean container from one working day to the next. Washed with soap and rinsed in very hot water, one container thus may be alternated with another until the egg mixture is depleted or noted to be verging upon putrefaction. Decomposition of egg is obviously telltale.

Egg, oil, and varnish combined Aside from egg itself, the most favored emulsion appears to be one which makes use of both an oil and a varnish together to vary the composition of the oil ingredient combined with egg. The formulation is based upon the combining in equal parts of whole egg and oily ingredient. The recipe may be represented as follows:

1 **whole egg**
stand oil, or boiled linseed, equal to 1/2 the volume of beaten egg
varnish, damar (or copal) equal to 1/2 the egg volume
water, equal to the combined volume of egg, varnish, and oil
oil of cloves, 3 drops

Converting the quantities into whole parts, the recipe may also be expressed according to the following proportions:

2 parts whole egg
4 parts water
1 part stand oil
1 part damar varnish
6 drops oil of cloves

Into a glass measuring cup, or any calibrated glass utensil, break one egg. Beat it well, either manually or mechanically. The oil and the varnish may be added in one bulk or a few drops at a time, accompanied by vigorous agitation in either case. The oil of cloves may also be added at this point.

The next step after the oily ingredient of the medium has been readied is the addition of water. Rather than add the full measure in one pouring, begin first with two or three drops, again stirring with gusto. With each successive addition, double the last amount until water and oily substances are completely emulsified. Strain as described. This medium can be expected to last for six months without refrigeration. Occasionally the ingredients will be noted to separate, but they will homogenize if shaken hard and well.

Commercial preparations   Egg emulsion preparations are available under only a few labels. Egg tempera colors, in tubes, may also be obtained. Yet, perhaps to assure control, and quite probably because of fascination and romanticism, most artists prefer to make their own emulsions.

Other modifications of media   All emulsions, including those not described in these pages, should be extended freely with water. Water quantity will vary with effect desired, and thinning does not alter the emulsion once it has been balanced.

Emulsions possess the ability to mix with oil-ground colors. This ability enables each to retain flow and smoothness. There are two ways of combining ingredients. Emulsion and oil color may be mixed together in the ratio of one part emulsion to two parts oil color. They may also be brought together during the painting process itself. Oil colors may be painted into sections of a painting still wet with tempera or temperas may be worked into wet oils. This process is referred to as "wet into wet" and is associated with fifteenth century German and Flemish techniques.

TEMPERA COLORS

The preparation of colors is also usually a hand process in the studio. With a muller, dry pigments are ground together with distilled water into a thick paste, somewhat the consistency of oil paints. The mix should be smooth and even. If pigments are not fine enough, they should be ground in a china mortar and pestle before being mulled. Most manufacturers of artists' colors package pigments in dry form. These should not be confused, however, with so-called powdered temperas, which are widely used in public and private schools. Neither should the studio mixture be confused with other tempera types, such as poster paints.

Kept in tightly closed containers, such as the screw-type or snap-lid kinds in which baby foods are sold, the pigment and distilled water mixture will last indefinitely. When the colors are to be used with egg yolk, they are mixed in equal volumes just before painting is about to proceed. Ordinarily the amounts should not exceed the color needs anticipated for the day. The painting technique employed will also govern quantities prepared.

When an egg-oil-varnish medium is to be used, it may be added when making the pigment solution. *The amount is far less than when yolk only is added.* For each ounce of pigment volume, add five drops of emulsion. During the process of painting more emulsion will be added to the mixture when it is taken up by brushes dipped into emulsion beforehand.

The pigment paste may be kept in lidless containers if necessary or if adjudged preferable. A layer of distilled water serves well as a seal to prevent drying. However, if unattended, this cover will evaporate; it must be replaced every several months to remove dust and other bits of matter which might have fallen into the container. Improvising an additional cover is an obvious recourse. Any rust-resistant material, such as glass, can easily be laid over the mouth of the container. Another worthwhile practice is to cover each pigment container by inverting a larger container over it.

The proper amount of egg or emulsion mixed with pigment can be determined by simple testing. One test is to allow a mixture to dry on the palette or on some similar surface. If a part of this sample is moistened with water, there should be no difference in its shade from that of the dry section. When egg yolk is used as the binder, another test can be used to indicate whether or not there is too much of it in color mixtures. If the sample is scraped with a palette knife it will either lift away as an oily shaving or it will flake. The former indicates a good balance, the latter requires the addition of more egg. Usually the amount of pigment paste and yolk are equal. Dull and chalky strokes require more egg. When a stroke is very shiny, the mixture needs more ground color. Strokes which dry with a slight gloss are satisfactory, although ideal mixtures do not shine when dry.

FINISHES FOR EGG TEMPERA

Varnishes are not necessary for the protection of paintings in egg. When perfectly dry, a most beautiful sheen is obtained if buffed with silk or any other cloth free of lint. The imperviousness of egg tempera to physical change from all of the usual conditions affecting other painting media is one of its notable features. The criteria for the framing of oil paintings are proper for tempera works. Glass is not needed, as it is for watercolor.

PASTEL PAINTING

Pastel painting is a rather unusual member of the watercolor family. It is what might be called a dry technique—one which does not require a solvent. In common with watercolor, pastel has a binder and depends on the surface quality of the support for effects. Not too old a technique, pastels have been used quite widely since the eighteenth century; they were originally a medium for portraiture, but are now employed virtually without restriction.

Pastel should not be confused with other preparations which bear physical resemblances to it. The finest is a mixture of pigment and gum tragacanth molded into sticks or cakes. It is soft and fragile, since very little binder is used. Proper depositing of color depends upon the ease with which pigments are loosened during use; the separating of pigment particles into a free state is similar to the same principle associated with transparent watercolor. Also added to pastel preparations is whiting or pipe-clay, an inert substance which serves as a filler to impart opacity or covering powers. The characteristic pale and soft coloration of pastels is imparted by the whiting. Other kinds of preparations are less satisfactory. Chalk crayons, for example, use either an oil or a wax as a binder and are much too hard as a result. There are also some commercial "pastels" which are really chalks that have been dyed. These are not color-fast, nor are they as delicate and rich as true pastels. Superior pastels are luminous no matter how they are handled.

Pigment is discharged from the pastel stick by the wearing action of the ground. Pastel grounds require sufficient tooth to loosen pigment with a scraping or abrasive action. Not all surfaces are suitable, and specially prepared grounds are usually necessary. These are available commercially in paper or canvas form. The better grades of charcoal paper are also occasionally recommended. There are some artists who prefer to customize desired surfaces themselves. In most instances the surface to be treated is brushed with gum water and then sprinkled with finely ground pumice stone. Maurice de la Tour, a master of pastel during the rococo period, is said to have used smalt for this purpose successfully. Smalt is a cobalt blue glass or frit which has been used as a ceramics coloring ingredient since Egyptian times. It is coarse and provides a tinted ground in spite of its lack of tinctorial power. Tinted or toned grounds occur often with pastel painting.

A firm support is desirable. Quite often papers are pasted to linen or canvas backings which have been mounted on stretchers or on composition board, such as millboard or masonite. The steps which describe the procedure for the mounting of rice papers (see Chapter 5) are just as useful in this instance. Instructions for the classic English method of mounting finished water colors may be followed for the mounting of papers or canvas which have been treated for additional tooth without having been stretched first. Various sanding papers or cloths can be used as grounds, but they are not generally satisfactory because of too obvious coarseness, ground tone, and limited size. Convenient to prepare, however, are cardboard or wallboard supports which are coated with a mixture of lacquer or paint and pumice, silica, or similar grit materials in heaping proportion.

The fragile mien of pastel predetermines much of its expressive uses and techniques. Lightness of touch in handling and airiness of appearance are generally the bases of style. Elusive, shimmering veils of color are its most valuable effects. The range of contrasts possible for value and color is limited, due to the presence of the whiting binder. Most exponents of pastel prefer to accept this limitation, regarding it more as an advantage. Others, unfortunately, are inclined to apply prevailing painting techniques, without regard as to whether or not the medium is adaptable or appropriate to the means. Indeed, pastel is sometimes used in bravura terms, with bold strokes or other manual accoutrements dominating the art scene at any given time. A Bach partita played by a string quartet is right and natural, but a quartet rendering a full-scale symphony would amount to little more than the whistling of a tune, so to speak. Pastel is not a universal medium.

Pastels lend themselves to either graphic or drawing effects. The first evidence of this use may be seen in examples of fifteenth- and sixteenth-century drawings done in red chalk—the agreed forerunner of pastels—or silverpoint. These sketches, portraits mostly, were colored with a form of pastel. Built-up, or "painterly," working of pastel is a later development which is more usually favored. In this technique the color and grain of the support are less prominent, and coverage of area is greater, as is the employment of successive layerings of color. A system of lightly laying one color over another yields numerous and beautiful variations which can be achieved only by pastels. In their use of areas consisting of broken color, loosely dispersed pigments reflecting light simultaneously, the impressionists show that they understood this quality, especially Edgar Degas and Mary Cassatt.

The usual approach in pastels consists of laying in the design with several colors which are rubbed with the finger or, better, with a stump, such as is used in charcoal drawing. Stiff bristle brushes may also be used to spread or fuse color into place. In principle this step corresponds to the use of neutral tints in transparent watercolor paintings, or to grisaille stages in other painting techniques—notably egg tempera and oil. Black, white, and carmine were customarily used in the eighteenth century for this phase. When a generalized image has been established, final touches are added, bringing the work into clearer focus. These touches remain as applied—direct, not rubbed. No rules govern the proportion of the painting which is rubbed or directly done. As needs arise, choices become self-evident. Of course, pastels may be used in an entirely direct manner, without preliminary sketches or the use of "dead coloring" as described above. The important advantage of direct application, again, is the brilliance and sparkle imparted by the combination of pigment and ground bodies which reflect light.

Pastels are not without disadvantages, one of which is the lack of deep darks and of strength of value contrasts. Because of whiting in all pastel colors—including the darkest—it is not possible to secure deep darks over areas already covered by lighter pastels. Therefore, to best manage darks it is advisable to begin paintings with the darkest colors first. Correcting the work for any reason is also difficult, and too much rubbing deadens the painting. When allowed to come in contact with the fingers, the ground becomes oily. Some painters will not handle the support or the unframed finished work without wearing clean gloves. Furthermore, unless the painting has been fixed, ordinary handling is often sufficient to loosen the paint from the surface. Shaking or "dusting" off may be eliminated by spraying the work with a fixative, often shellac dissolved in alcohol. Synthetic fixatives made especially for pastels are also available. Some artists spray individual layers of pastel as a painting progresses. Unfortunately, while bonding pastels to the support, fixatives cause pigments to become transparent, thus minimizing color brilliancy. Given a choice between fixing or preserving the best color properties, the latter is often elected. If fixative is to be applied, it is important to maintain the painting or drawing in a flat, horizontal position. Care should be taken that the atomizer, blower, or spray container is held in the proper position and at the distance recommended for the emission of a uniformly fine spray. The support will collect the fixative as it settles in a fine mist to the surface of the work. To assure a depositing throughout, spraying should be directed beyond the painting's edges, and the motion, or stroke, of spraying should be made with even passes. Unfixed pastels may be kept stored in a horizontal position on top of one another if liners of cellophane or similar material are used for separating them. Pastel paintings may be kept in this way safely until such time as they are to be fixed or framed. Pastels are framed in the same manner and for the same reasons as transparent watercolors.

Combinations of pastels with other media are not unusual. Actually, they are often applied to paintings and drawings which are begun with watercolor, gouache, or ink. A good balance between pastel and the companion medium is essential. If used sparingly, however, pastels contribute little to the union. This is most noticeable in the company of transparent watercolor, particularly when touches are meant to correct or revive a part gone awry. Mixed media techniques are more successful when each component complements the other, or when there is a definite plan of synthesis from the start. Unique unto itself, pastel also has the virtue of being compatible with other media.

CHAPTER 3

Color, Pigments, Palettes

COLOR

Response to color is a basic part of the act of seeing.
It is color which attracts the attention to the presence and
generalized appearance of objects in the environment;
impressions of differences in forms, line, texture, and value
come only with further looking. For example, the
blue, white, and black of a nut-hatch winding a path
against the red tinges and gray-greens of an oak's
lichen-mottled bark are perceived before the identification
of a particular bird and a particular tree is completed.
Painting concerns itself with the use of color. A knowledge
of the various means of color representation is a
necessity to the serious painter. It is therefore important
to become aware of the physical
and expressive characteristics of coloring agents.

PIGMENTS

All painting media consist of pigments in combination with a binder. Pigments are transparent particles of matter which assume color property by means of selective absorption of the component colors of white light. Physically, white light contains all colors of the visible spectrum. A red pigment is a tiny body which transmits a red color because its structure allows light rays of the red region of the spectrum to pass through it. The same holds true, of course, with blues and yellows. The light-bending power of a transparent pigment particle is called its *refractive index.* The amount of light which is reflected by any given pigment and its covering power are determined by its refractive index. (Covering power is the ability of a pigment when made into paint to cover the surface over which it is applied.) Pigments reflect more light when surrounded by air than when bounded by binders, but binders with a low refractive index help pigments to retain more of their true color. The hiding power is usually greatest among pigments compounded of the heavy metals; in contrast to these, the transparent lake pigments exert very little hiding power. Transparent pigments are acceptable in water color painting, for transparency is one of its distinguishing features. In other vehicles, transparent paints are acceptable for glazing techniques.

Pigment grains vary in size and shape. The smoothness, evenness, and uniformity of film of a paint is dependent upon the size and uniformity of pigment grains. Fine and uniform size assure a uniform paint. These traits are important more for commercial paints than for artists' watercolors; in fact, the coarseness and graininess of larger and irregular particles are quite desirable. Early Chinese paintings possess a unique beauty, thanks to imperfectly ground pigments. Generally speaking, the finer and smaller the particle size, the softer the color usually is and the better the tonal quality.

Purity and strength are also characteristic of good pigments. High strength and good tinctorial value (also called *body*) are diminished when the pigment is adulterated by inert fillers, such as talc. Thus, public school powdered pigments should not be used for this reason, particularly when painting in egg tempera.

The tonal quality of a pigment is a subtle quality which imparts a soft and rich color clarity (top-tone) together with solid depth (undertone).

The most important practical characteristic of any pigment is its degree of permanence when suspended in a vehicle as a paint. Factors which may affect durability are:

1. Reaction to light;
2. Reaction to atmospheric impurities and moisture;
3. Reaction to vehicle or medium;
4. Reaction to other pigments when intermixed.

Inquiry into the origins of artists' pigments is fascinating. Coloring matter has been scraped from the earth's crust, squeezed from vegetation, extracted from animals, and precipitated synthetically in the chemist's laboratory. With man's entry into the realms of outer space, even more wondrous pigment substances are likely to be discovered. All known pigments are divided into two classifications: the inorganic and the organic pigments.

the inorganic pigments

The inorganic pigments are color agents which are not in chemical union with carbon. They are obtained from nonliving matter. The most common of such pigments occur plentifully in the form of minerals, ores, and sedimentary clays deposited in the earth's crust; these are the so-called "natural" pigments. Other inorganic pigments are those synthetically produced from the heavy metals.

For convenience of classification, the inorganic pigments may be subdivided into three categories:

1. Mineral colors;
2. Metallic oxides;
3. Blacks.

MINERAL COLORS

Mineral colors, the first type of inorganic pigments, are made up of complex mineral mixtures typified by those natural pigments which we know as the oxides, the ochres, the siennas, and the umbers. These form the basic group of earth colors. In this classification also belong the mineral pigments; however, it is well to avoid confusion in terminology. Strictly speaking, unlike earths and clays, mineral pigments are chemical compounds which are definite in physical form and constant in chemical behavior. Examples of true mineral pigments are those derived from *lapis lazuli* (natural ultramarine), orpiment (King's yellow), and azurite (mountain blue).

METALLIC OXIDES

The metallic oxides are manufactured from metals. As the term implies, they are combinations of metals and oxides. Naples Yellow, for example, is a chemical compound of lead and antimony oxides. The best known metallic oxides are those made from cadmium, chromium, cobalt, copper, iron, manganese, mercury, nickel, selenium, tin, titanium, and zinc.

INORGANIC BLACKS

The third order of inorganic colors are the blacks. These consist of the mineral blacks, iron oxide, and manganese dioxide, which are also listed as metallic oxides. This dual classification is for the purpose of providing an inorganic counterpart to the organic blacks.

the organic pigments   Organic pigments are chemical compounds of carbon combined with hydrogen, nitrogen, oxygen, sulphur, or other elements. They have been primarily derived from vegetable sources, and occasionally from animal matter. Indigo, madder, and saffron have long been important vegetable colors. Indian Yellow (puree) was once separated from the urine of cows in India, but is now manufactured synthetically.

The most important of the organic pigments are the synthetic varieties. By and large, they exhibit more permanent characteristics than do the natural organic colorants. In general, however, the organic pigments are markedly fugitive, and impermanent. Synthetic organic colors are compounds called anilines or coal-tars. Artificial alizarin, magenta, and toluidine red are the typical aniline colors.

Most natural organic pigments are not used today other than in primitive cultures. In subdividing organic pigments into color groups, therefore, natural coloring matter is omitted. The organic pigment types are (1) the aniline colors (2) the lakes, and (3) the blacks.

THE ANILINES

The anilines are made by complicated chemical processes from the distillation products of coal tar, a byproduct of coke and coal gas manufacture. Coal-tar compounds contain chiefly carbon, hydrogen, nitrogen, and, at times, sulphur. Aniline manufacturing techniques produce colors in dry powder form, which result in deep, rich shades when dissolved in water or organic solvents, such as alcohol, acetone, or benzol. In this physical condition the anilines can be used as dyestuffs.

THE LAKES

The lakes are a group of colors which are really modified anilines converted from a dye state into pigment form. To achieve paint qualities, aniline dyes are precipitated onto inorganic bases, such as calcium sulphate, *blanc-fixe* (barite, barium white), and aluminum hydrate. Calcium sulphate and aluminum hydrate are insoluble, semitransparent, finely divided, and inert. When they are used as bases or substrates, the resulting paints are essentially tinctorial and transparent. Barite (or barytes), tin oxide, and zinc oxide most often serve as the substrates to obtain pigments with body and hiding power from the lakes.

Depending upon the bases used, the same dye can be made to produce lakes of different hues and shades. Stable lakes are not available in all colors, however. Lakes in the red shade of the spectrum are reasonably permanent, and there is every reason to believe that the dependability of lakes in the other spectrum regions will improve. The phthalocyanine blues and the Hansa yellows have already successfully established themselves as permanent.

Organic Blacks

The organic blacks—carbon black, lamp black, and vine black—are pure carbon colors which are exceptionally permanent. All of them are manufactured products. Carbon black is carbon precipitated out of the partial burning of natural gas, oil, wood, and other organic materials. Lamp black is precipitated from the condensed smoke of burning mineral oil, tar, pitch, or resin; it is almost a pure carbon. The burning of bones is the means of manufacturing vine black, as is the burning or carbonizing of vegetable substances which produces a vine black similar to charcoal. Vine sticks or vine wood have been a perennial source, which accounts for the names of this carbon-type black. Other vegetable blacks have been obtained from peach stones, cork, and coconut husks.

The amount and particle size of amorphous carbon present in the organic black pigments affect the strength and shade of each. Carbon black is both harder and more granular than lamp black, for example, and it wets more readily in water. Neither is a true black in color: carbon black has a deep brownish tinge, while lamp black and vine black are somewhat bluish. Excellent neutral grays and bluish grays come from mixtures of lamp black and vine black, respectively.

chemical behavior of pigments   A certain degree of permanence and fastness of color is expected in artist-grade pigment preparations. Resistance to light, heat, water, and erosion are necessary to assure stability. The more chemically inert a pigment is, the stronger is its resistance to changes caused by the presence of light, air, and moisture in the environment. Therefore, in the interest of a painting's longevity, a brief review of color stability as influenced by light, heat, moisture, and air may prove helpful. A moment of close observation should also establish reasons for the design and construction of picture frames detailed later.

Light

Some colors are prone to dimming, darkening, and browning when subject to light. Through photochemical reactions, strong sunlight is known not only to cause such effects but to produce actual change in the color of some pigments as well. The effect of light is most noticeable in the "fading" exhibited by organic dyestuffs. The same is true of the lakes and of zinc oxide when they are used in the form of paled tints. Whenever moisture and heat are present with light, the rates of color degradation and discoloration are increased.

AIR

Chemical pollution of the atmosphere also contributes to discoloration problems. Industrial gas discharges contain hydrogen sulphide and sulphur dioxide, which, combined with atmospheric oxygen, react chemically with some pigments to cause discoloration and fading. Copper and lead pigments are susceptible to these effects under certain conditions, and the gum binders of watercolors do not afford adequate covering and protection for pigment particles. Pigments bounded by oil and hardened into film are far less likely to be affected by sulphides.

MOISTURE

The presence of moisture has been noted in most instances of pigments undergoing color changes. Its exact role has not been determined, but it is believed to serve as a catalytic agent. When moisture is excluded under experimental conditions, chemical reactions involved in fading and discoloration are retarded. Water color gums may lose adhesive powers whenever humid conditions prevail.

pigment admixtures

Exposure of paintings to light and atmosphere is unavoidable, but simple measures of precaution can minimize the probability of chemical alteration of pigments. When certain pigments are mixed together, the resulting combinations prove chemically unstable. Little if anything can be done to regain the color quality present when first mixed. This is true of some oxygen-bearing pigments— the chromates, for example—which become altered through a loss of oxygen when combined with some of the organic pigments. The direct combination of the sulphides with copper and lead pigments produces brown or black copper and lead sulphides. Intermixings of the simple oxide pigments—the sulphates, the phosphates, and the carbonates—are safe, causing no undesirable reactions. Binders, too, may be a cause for some color changes. Because of their sulphur content, egg vehicles, for example, can affect some of the blues.

No admixtures suffer more serious effects than those containing emerald green; in fact, one cannot overemphasize how important it is to bear in mind its far-reaching capacity to affect a number of colors. Emerald green (Veronese green)—an inorganic prepared from copper, acetic acid, white arsenic, and sodium carbonate—blackens in contact with sulphurous air and pigments. Emerald green must not be mixed, therefore, with any of the sulphide colors: the cadmium yellows and red, vermilion, ultramarine, King's yellow (orpiment), Naples yellow, and permanent blue (ultramarine light). Beyond its unpopularity for mixing purposes, emerald green is also not recommended for reasons more grave. It is poisonous and, in watercolors, not stable enough to be worth the risk. King's yellow, a sulphide of arsenic, is also best eliminated because of its poisonous traits. Fortunately, it is seldom available because of its rarity.

selecting watercolor pigments   Manufacturers of colors engage in continuous research programs to improve paints. Important substitutes have been artificially produced, particularly in the realm of the organic pigments. Artificial alizarin (alizarin crimson) is superior to natural alizarin (madder) in being more light-fast and capable of providing more shades of red. Also synthetically produced but of less technological significance are the Mars colors—Mars yellow, Mars orange, Mars red, and Mars violet. Excellent though they may be for homogeneity and fineness of grain, they hold no real edge over the natural yellow and red iron earths. Nonetheless, these developments are indicative of efforts to perfect new and better color products. Consequently, claims of quality and permanence put forth by makers of the better-known brands may be taken in good faith.

At this point a listing of watercolors would seem to be appropriate. We have seen that colors are rated in terms of permanence, based upon ability to withstand physical changes. In this compilation individual colors will be grouped under headings derived from their response to light, air, and moisture. The first group identifies those colors which are unaffected by environmental factors. In most instances additional notes relevant to color traits may appear.

I. PIGMENTS REGARDED AS ABSOLUTELY PERMANENT

(unaffected by sunlight, atmosphere, and dampness)

Burnt Sienna
an earth, calcined sienna

Burnt Umber
an earth, calcined umber, slightly redder than umber

Cerulean Blue
the only cobalt blue without a violet tint; difficult to use in washes

Charcoal Gray

Chinese White (Zinc White)

Cobalt Blue (Thenard's Blue)
a costly color; inexpensive preparations are adulterated or substituted with ultramarine and blue lakes

Cobalt Violet
a reddish violet; costly; transparent and weak in tinting strength; should not be touched by metals

Davy's Gray

Indian Red (Rouge, Colcothar, Caput Mortuum)
dark red oxide; excellent hiding power

Ivory Black (Bone Black)
most intense of the blacks

Lamp Black (Carbon Black)
bluish cast, excellent for neutral grays

Lemon Yellow (Barium Yellow, Strontium Yellow, Permanent Yellow)
a pale green-yellow which may turn slightly greener upon being exposed to light

Light Red (Venetian Red)
light warm red ochre; calcined yellow ochre

Oxide of Chromium (Chromium Oxide Green, Opaque)
dull green; most stable of the greens; coarse and irregular pigment particles

Raw Sienna
an earth, a yellow ochre

Raw Umber
a warm, reddish-brown earth with a greenish undercast

Terre Verte (Green Earth)
a neutral sage green; low hiding power; long used as a flesh-tone foundation

Viridian (Emeraude Green, Emerald Oxide of Chromium, Transparent Oxide of Chromium, Verte Emeraude, Guignet's Green)
a deep cool green, excellent tinting strength and transparency, and a replacement for toxic emerald green

Yellow Ochre (Ochre)
natural earth, occurs in a color range from dull, pale yellow to reddish brown; good hiding power

II. PIGMENTS REGARDED AS ABSOLUTELY PERMANENT BUT WHICH MIGHT BE AFFECTED BY

(a. *atmospheric acids and sulphides*)

Ultramarine, natural

Ultramarine, artificial (French blue, French ultramarine, New Blue, Permanent Blue, Ultramarine Ash Blue)
(ultramarines should not be mixed with alizarin lakes and chrome yellows. Don't use in tempera; use Monastral.)

(b. *sunlight*)

Mineral Violet (Permanent Mauve, Permanent Violet)
weak in tinting strength

Vermilion (Cinnabar, English Vermilion, Chinese Vermilion)
strong sunlight causes darkening; often substituted by cadmium red; ancient and popular red; good watercolor should not be mixed with Prussian blue and tempera

(c. *dampness*)

Cadmium Yellow (Cadmium Yellow Lithopone, Orient Yellow)
  shades range from lemon yellow to orange

Cobalt Green (Zinc Green, Rinmann's Green)
  a bluish green; semitransparent; average hiding power

Cobalt Yellow(Aureolin)
  don't use in tempera

Mineral Violet

III. DURABLE BUT LESS THAN PERMANENT PIGMENTS

(a. *not affected by light, atmosphere, or moisture*)

Cadmium Lemon
  light shade of cadmium yellow

Cadmium Orange
  a modification of cadmium yellow

Cadmium Yellow, Pale

Cadmium Yellow, Deep

Cadmium Red

Cadmium Red, Deep

Cadmium Scarlet
  (the cadmiums should not be used with Prussian blue)

Harrison Red (Toluidine Red)
  a brilliant red lake; will stain superimposed color; avoid mixing
  with ochres and siennas

Hooker's Green, Dark

Hooker's Green, Light
  both are really mixtures of Prussian blue and gamboge; may
  turn to blue if gamboge fades

Indian Yellow
  translucent, deep, rich orange color

Indigo, artificial

blue and green in thin layers; fair tinting strength, good in watercolor and tempera; replaces woad

Madder Lake (Rose Madder Genuine)

made from madder root; more orange and red than artificial alizarin because of the purpurin contained

Manganese Blue (Mineral Blue)

a green-blue pigment, weak in tinting and hiding power; very inert chemically

New Gamboge

Olive Green

Phthalocynine Blue (Monastral Blue)

artificial dyestuff with very strong tinctorial properties; exerts twice the strength of Prussian blue and twenty to forty times the depth of ultramarine. This power can contaminate other colors on a palette easily, so it is wise to isolate it when painting. It is the purest known blue. Precaution should be taken also with Phthalocynine Green.

Scarlet Lake

Sepia

Sepia, Warm

black or dark brown secretion from ink sac of the cuttle-fish or squid; high tinctorial power; fairly permanent under ordinary conditions; easy to wash

(b. *durable pigments which are lessened in stability when used in thin washes or when used with Chinese white*)

Alizarin Carmine (Madder Carmine or Alizarin)

Alizarin Crimson (Permanent Crimson, Ruby Madder, or Alizarin)

Brown Madder (Alizarin)

Madder Carmine (Alizarin)

Neutral Tint

Payne's Gray

Rose Madder (Alizarin)

(the alizarins should not be mixed with ultramarines)

(c. durable pigments which are darkened
by a sulphurous atmosphere)

Chrome Orange
lead chromate in the chrome yellow family; other yellows are
better

Naples Yellow (Antimony Yellow)
lead and antimony oxides

(d. durable pigments which fade in light
but recover in darkness)

Cyanine Blue (Leitch's Blue)
Prussian Blue (Chinese Blue, Antwerp Blue, Paris Blue, Berlin
Blue)

IV. SEMIDURABLE COLORS

Crimson Lake (Carmine Lake, Cochineal)
a natural organic dyestuff made from the dried bodies of the
female insect, *Coccus Cacti*; turns brownish and fades rapidly
in strong sunlight

Purple Lake
a modified crimson lake

Gamboge
a yellow gum resin; fades rapidly in sunlight; fugitive in thin
washes

Hooker's Green, Light

Sap Green
a natural organic dyestuff; made from juice of ripened buck-
thorn berries

Prussian Green (Chrome Green)
mixture of Prussian blue and chrome yellow; fugitive in thin
washes

Rose Dore

Violet Carmine

V. FUGITIVE COLORS

> **Carmine**
>
> **Chrome Lemon**
>
> **Chrome Yellow**
>
> **Mauve**
>
> **Rose Carthame**
>
> **Van Dyke Brown**

A BASIC PALETTE

Not all of the colors just surveyed are necessary for any single palette. In many ways, the fewer one uses, the better. Actually, as few as five different colors can suffice: light red, Prussian blue, burnt sienna, yellow ochre, and ivory black. Each is stable and reasonably permanent. Such a palette would, however, be truly minimal—a palette devoid of brilliant reds and yellows. A basic palette might consist of the following selections:

Reds
Light red (Venetian, Indian, Tusian, Mars)
Cadmium Red
Madder (natural alizarin)

Yellows
Cobalt yellow (Aureolin) affected by dampness
Yellow ochre
Raw Sienna

Blues
Cobalt blue
very stable; unaffected by sunlight; a pure shade of blue; very workable in washes
Ultramarine artificial
avoid with tempera; don't use with chrome yellow or artificial alizarin
Prussian

Greens
 Viridian

Blacks
 Ivory black

The colors of this limited palette are compatible with one another. Other pigments may be reviewed to supplement the selection, either to extend the color range or to substitute in some instances for pigment on this list. Phthalocynine blue is often preferred to Prussian blue, in spite of its phenomenal strength and the difficulty of preventing it from sullying other colors in the same palette; it should be used sparingly, however. Raw sienna sometimes is found offensive because of its assertive rawness.

Of course, other reasons influence palette modifications, including human weaknesses and curiosity. Vermilion, in spite of its tendency to blacken, is beautiful and difficult to resist. Hooker's green, dark, has a power and richness of its own which is worth the risk of possible fading. To increase the range of blacks and grays, Payne's gray, Davy's gray and neutral tint are often favored. And so it goes. On the other hand, one very valid reason for modifying a palette occurs with landscape problems, where some colors will be found to be more gratifying and appropriate than others. Color preferences often correspond to seasonal changes to a great degree.

No comment has been made about white as part of this basic watercolor palette. This omission is intentional because the lightening of watercolors is dependent upon allowing the whiteness of the paper ground to show through transparent paint layers. Colored washes and white paper are optical mixings. When a pigment white is added to the palette, one is working not in watercolor but in gouache.

PACKAGING OF WATERCOLORS

Watercolors are commercially available in the form of cakes, pans, and tubes. Cakes are a hardened, dry preparation; pigments in pans are semimoist and are kept in small porcelain cups. The more popular moist colors are sealed in metal tubes. Each of these forms has its own special advantage to the user. One significant advantage of watercolor cakes, for instance, is that they appear to work better in washes than pigments ground in other consistencies. Pan colors manufactured in the Orient are somewhat coarse in grain, partly because of the grind and the addition of kaolin. They are useful for effects of graininess.

INKS

Inks are associated with watercolor methods in a number of ways. They have been used and still occur as a regular part of the palette for both transparent and opaque painting. And, of course, ink is a popular vehicle by itself, as a means for both drawing and painting.

India inks are the best known and most convenient. They are uniform in consistency and, as inks go, permanent. Because India inks are liquids, they should be kept tightly capped to avoid evaporation. When dry, India inks are waterproof, but they are not highly permanent; this is particularly true of the colored mixtures.

An old forerunner of India ink is the ink-stick. Originating in China, it is made of soot mixed with glue in a ratio of two parts soot to one part glue. This ink is called *Sumi* ink, a term which refers to its use in a Japanese painting style called *Sumi*. The soot (carbon) is obtained from kiln-burned pine or fir or from the burning of vegetable oil in an earthenware bowl. The mixture is molded into a cake, or stick, and left to dry. To produce ink, the stick must be rubbed with water on an inkstone, a hard block such as a ceramic tile. Because Chinese ink does not lose its gloss and its jet-black value, it is the best of inks. Oriental inks may also be obtained in liquid form.

Some variations in the tonality of Chinese ink mixes are produced by additives. Ground oyster shells are sometimes added to obtain a dull ink for various purposes. Colors, except for vermilion, are also added at times.

PALETTES

All watercolor palettes are made from nonabsorbent materials whose finishes are resistant to staining and chipping. The usual palette is made of metal, coated with a porcelain or baked enamel surface. There is a choice of sizes. The smaller are usually fitted into sketch boxes, to be unfolded when needed, and the larger are available singly, independent of kits. Also favored is the color plate, made of white, glazed porcelain. This type is practical, but limited in the size of its mixing well. Somewhat less expensive, pressed plastic modifications have reached the market. These are serviceable and have deeper paint wells than most palettes. They are light, flexible, and hold their shape well.

In their basic design, watercolor palettes are flat surfaces which are divided into areas reserved for the mixing of paints and wells, or reservoirs, for the storage of colors. The wells are usually regularly spaced depressions. In some designs, both mixing areas and wells are recessed, separated into compartments by walls. This version is preferable for keeping colors and mixtures from contaminating each other too easily. Wells are distributed around the perimeter of the palette, although quite often they are incorporated along one edge only. The porcelain water dish is round, consisting of a water well at its center and surrounded by wells, usually eight. Slightly over five inches in diameter, they provide limited mixing area, particularly when compared to rectangular palettes measuring 12 to 16 inches. Usually available with the color plate is a matching three-compartment water dish, of porcelain also. The color plate fits over the top of the water dish when it is not in use.

Palettes are white for good reason. The purpose is to simulate the whiteness of most watercolor papers, enabling better approximations of color qualities desired in the painting. Being transparent, watercolor pigments would not show up faithfully if mixed on dark surfaces.

In choosing a palette, structural considerations should be applied.

The enameled metal palettes tend to warp out of plane, due to tension between the base metal and its coating. The gauge of the metal is usually too light. Irregularities of plane in the vicinity of mixing areas cause color mixtures to run or drain across the palette and into the color wells. Pressed plastic and ceramic plates are safe from this fault. In the interest of any palette, there are some instructions in common. When cleaning palettes use water only, and if color needs to be loosened, use a sponge, a rag or a brush. Avoid steelwool, scouring powders, and other abrasives. The same may be said of scrapers, nails, or other sharp instruments. If paints other than those binded in gum are used, such as casein, do not let these dry or harden on the palette. Removal is difficult, and frequently it is at the cost of lifting chips of enameling which did not release from hardened paint. Good results depend on good care of materials.

CHAPTER 4

Sketching and Subject Matter

Sketching is regarded as a necessary phase of painting. As a guide and as a means of establishing objectives, sketching helps to establish plans for action. Developed into a habit, sketching sharpens the abilities to observe and to convert that which is noted into pictorial existence. During preliminary stages the essentials of content, visual order, and technical treatment are confronted, stimulating the imagination and arousing purposeful concentration.

Artists have employed several ways of keeping notes as a reservoir of information. Free-hand drawing, the camera, and contemplative study act as conveyors of impressions and thought. While the camera and reflective thinking both serve conveniently, neither is truly useful until transplanted into a form of drawing.

Eventually it is a drawing that breaks ground for a painting.

In its close relationship to painting, three functions may be ascribed to drawing, each according to time of occurrence.

The most evident of these is the preliminary study—an initial trial which forecasts a painting's general organization. Usually such a sketch is restricted in its detailing and execution, with focus on the more structural features of composition, distribution of values, and color notations—in short, generalized order. As drawings begin to separate from the more rudimentary plan inclusive of them all, elements to be emphasized in the painting are frequently rendered more meticulously. A closer study of a weed, for instance, may prove the difference between an unrealized and a superior landscape. Many are the landscapes which fail from ignorance of the growth of grass or the shape of a pebble!

By and large, preparatory sketches are done in media other than watercolor. Pencil, pen, charcoal, crayon, pastel—any and all—are common choices. In scale, drawings vary from the condensed size of the so-called "thumbnails" to schemes at least as large as the projected painting. The advantage to be gained from large sketches is an experience which rehearses motions and suggests the qualities of brushwork to appear later. As a further reminder of effects to come, written notes often appear with drawings, referring to color combinations and mixings, to conditions of wetness to be introduced to areas of the painting, and to other aspects which will be significant in the final outcome. Not to be overlooked, however, is the employment of watercolors or inks for meeting the ends of sketching.

While some artists confine their studies entirely to free-hand forms, others depend in part upon carrying a camera in addition to sketch pads wherever curiosity leads them to wander. During short stays in a locality, for instance, the camera proves an efficient time-saver which captures more of places, things, and people than do other methods. Direct copying of photographic data, assembled in this way is tempting, but the painter who is honestly offended by this thought, will confine himself to the more legitimate applications of his photographs. Turning to photographs to freshen the memory and for more intensive study of details provokes no quarrel, but relying upon photographs entirely, to the point of straining for the

Artist: *JOHN SINGER SARGENT*
Title: *Carrara: A Quarry*
Medium: Watercolor

Sometimes painters who are known for their work in other media turn to watercolor for any of several reasons. Watercolor is a reminder to look for the spontaneous and natural qualities of one's usual medium. Notes for works in oil often are made in watercolor. Artists of the past recorded their travels in sketch form, and this particular work was probably such a record.

closest duplication, is contrary to both creative fortitude and the capacities of the medium. Watercolors, especially, are thwartingly unmanageable for the copyist, and perhaps deservedly so.

When not occupied in collecting notes in visible ways, perceptive artists amass and solve the complex problems involved in lending expression through their paintings by the power of thinking. Letting nothing escape their attention without looking for explanations for all that is to be seen, they collect those endless facts of the commonplace which transcend themselves into new meanings. Everywhere, at all times, figments of paintings begin to take shape from something noticed and felt to be significant. Without moments of thought and the luxury of productive idleness, the elusiveness of truth and poetry in all things is likely to be missed. Painting from an engrossed memory quite often minimizes the need for detailed drawings beforehand, for the artist has, so to speak, already gotten down to the bones which support the process to follow. A direct and spontaneous flavor usually is distinctively evident in such an instance.

After a painting has been begun, sometimes a pause may become necessary to consider problems of amplification which might arise. Some part of the watercolor may not be progressing satisfactorily, or an impasse may be encountered because of insufficient prior analysis. At this point drawing may be renewed as a salvaging effort, provided the painting is in a stage which will bear a short wait. In effect, this is a brief return to preliminary-stage sketching. If quick trials bring about an adjustment of troublesome relationships, the painting is resumed. However, many painters, strongly acclimated to drawn forms, depend upon drawing techniques to advance the progress of their work throughout the painting process. Drawing and painting are virtually one and the same. Secondary drawing, as it might be called, therefore serves two purposes.

A finished painting does not necessarily complete the thought with which it was initially concerned. A whole new series of drawings may be prompted—some to reinterpret the original, if the artist feels it has fallen short of its goal; others to sound out further thematic variations. While reinforcing ideas and distilling imagery, sketching is, then, also a scale for evaluation.

THE STILL LIFE

The classic introductory problem to the practice of sketching and painting is the still life. As a means of training the eye, still life is regarded as essential to the understanding of the structure of objects and the principles by which they are represented. The elements of design, the rules of perspective, and techniques of rendering are incorporated into still life exercises.

Still life exercises have been criticized often because of the strong emphasis upon the mechanics of the representation of objects. These objections are not meant to discredit the value of the information gained so much as to question the failure to develop the other senses and interpretive attitudes. Expressive qualities, or meanings beyond pure representation, are conspicuously absent in most still life paintings.

The major fault of still life is not with its intent so much as with the static and contrived examples employed again and again. A triangle of cloth, faultlessly folded behind a plate beside a wine bottle, or a candlestick, and at least one more object, casually placed, have launched more hollow endeavors than, unfortunately, a Bach fugue. Many have been the books and ceramic cockatoos posed in little corners and shelves in homes and schools—little shrines to a muse surely long fled in disbelief. And think of the fish since Chardin and the apples after Cezanne!

As a pictorial end in itself, more often than not the still life will be a stilted affectation. If done as a study of familiar things as found in a natural relationship, much more meaning can be realized. A watercolor study of a hamburger sandwich by Oldenburg is a true depiction of a common edible, sensed and expressed in exquisitely beautiful color, wash, and mood. And how fragile, how subtly fleeting are poppies done by Hobson Pittman in pastels.

When planning a still life, the primary objective should be deciding the problem and what is to be learned from it in order to arrive at an expressive conclusion. The worth and value of the experience should extend itself as groundwork for subsequent applications.

THE FIGURE

Figure drawing, like still life, tends to follow some rather academic restrictions. There appears to be too much attention upon the posing of the figure, more for the sake of poses than for other intentions. Frequently the context within which figures are placed is overlooked. Alone, with no references to lend meaning to any given pose, the figure becomes forced and unconvincing.

Traditionally, figure studies focus upon the figure standing, sitting, and prone, with front, rear, and side views becoming the problem to be worked out. Sometimes props may be added, such as a bit of drapery, a chair, a rug—some touch of natural hominess. Who has not been confronted with a standing, seminude leaning on a pole and bulging with more muscle than even Michelangelo could have imagined? Unless a gondolier is intended, this is one of the more useless poses.

How should figures be studied? Draw them as they are—as people concerned with some significant activity. Use figures to express other things which represent human experience and condition. Compassion and empathy for man make the difference between the mediocre and the meaningful. How else can one account for a medieval *pietà*? Or a *Christina's World* (1948) by Andrew Wyeth? Or Ben Shahn's concern for Sacco and Vanzetti, and for the youth playing handball in New York's Lower East Side?

THE LANDSCAPE

Landscape concepts and watercolor media grew up together, so to speak, in the history of Western painting traditions. Both originated as formal elements at about the same time. Before the fifteenth century elements of landscape painting were seldom incorporated in

Artist: *ANDREE RUELLAN*
Title: *Date Seeds #2*
Medium: Watercolor on rice paper

Known for her sensitive draughtsmanship as a printmaker, Miss Ruellan puts this mastery into a deft and subtle study of a plant. An added softness of effect is contributed by the rice paper ground.

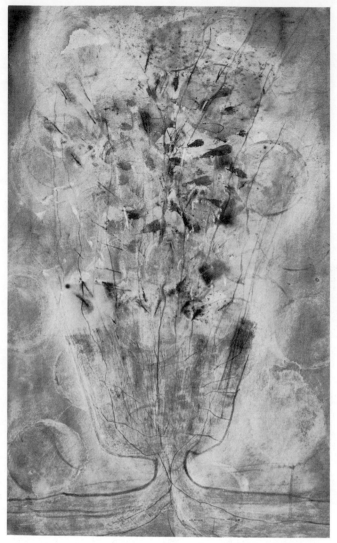

From the collection of the author

Artist: **DOUGLAS LOCKWOOD**
Title: *We Are Only The Medium Through Which It Flows*
Medium: Watercolor and ink

While this painting appears to be of flowers in a vase, it is meant to be more. We are the flowers, and it is we who are spiritually fed by mysterious taproots.

From a technical standpoint, painted layers have been rinsed off, then repainted and rinsed several times more, resulting in granulated effects. The linear treatment was drawn in part directly with a corner and edge of an ink stick and in part with a pen. Some spattering is included.

Artist: *ROBERT ANDREW PARKER*
Title: *Carmel Bedroom*
Medium: Watercolor

In this painting Robert Andrew Parker, a constant observer of all things, represents an interior, like one gigantic still life. It pulsates with an energy and freedom of adaptation to the medium to the point at which the technique becomes secondary to the topic and the artist's personality.

Artist: *ANDREW WYETH*
Title: *Benjamin's House*
Medium: Watercolor

A remarkable feature of this painting is that at first it appears to
have been executed with an eye toward faithful detailing, yet it consists of essentially three brush variations and three basic values. It is
pure brushwork. Any stroke taken out of this context would lose its
meaning. What appears to be a branch, for instance, would revert to
a fine flick of a line. This quiet study of the side of a house and a bit
of ground and undergrowth has all of the elements of a still life—
even though its subject is out-of-doors.

Artist: *WILLIAM KIENBUSCH*
Title: *New England Stove*
Medium: Gouache—collage

   The ornateness and basic geometric character of an old-fashioned kitchen stove is transformed into a pictorially geometric harmony. Formal perspective is not an element here, other than in a relative position. The stove top has been tilted into a perpendicular relationship to the frontal plane and base of the stove. The stovepipe overlaps one of the burners in an "x-ray" overlay.

Courtesy The Baltimore Museum of Art, Edward J. Gallagher III Memorial Collection

Artist: CHARLES DEMUTH
Title: *Bicycle Act—Vaudeville 1916*
Medium: Watercolor

With all of its "inaccuracies," this is a wonderful painting, which expresses the gesturings and maneuverings of a performer astride his trick bicycle. Distortions are evident here in relationships relative to the action, and not as a result of any lack of drawing skill—as the more familiar of Mr. Demuth's works will attest.

Artist: *ROBERT FREIMARK*
Title: *Figures on the Rocks*
Medium: Watercolor—drawing

Figures sunbathing in some isolated place are here combined into a landscape. Attention is called to the uses of line and wash. The picture is composed as a line drawing, but the lines do not dictate the placement of lights and darks, which are washed-in with a spontaneity which disregards the developing of the drawing's details.

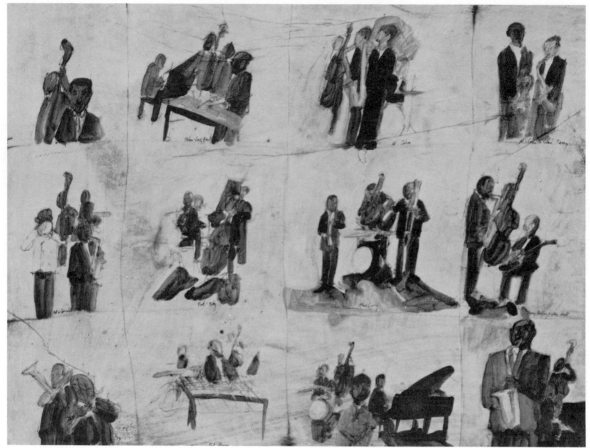

Artist: *ROBERT ANDREW PARKER*
Title: *Musicians 1963*
Medium: Watercolor

This composite of drawings depicting famous jazz musicians in live, on-the-spot sessions is originally from the artist's sketchbook. The sketching is extemporaneous and remarkably telling in the simplicity of its means. Among the groups and individuals pictured here are the Modern Jazz Quartet, Al Cohn and Clark Terry, Sonny Rollins and Jim Hall, Red Norvo, and Cannonball Adderley.

HOBSON PITTMAN, Summer Bouquet, 1962

The pastels of Hobson Pittman are delicately fused overlays of color. Lightly poised, form and space are suggested in a shimmering cascade of strokes, some large and direct, others trailing in fluid motions. Side by side, clear and clean, each blends with the other into a muted and atmospheric piece of a summer's day. While kept transparent in body and in conjunction with the ground tone, the manipulation of pastel here takes for its guide the qualities of brushwork exercised with the oil paintings of this master colorist.

ROBERT ANDREW PARKER, Vincent van Gogh in St. Remy

Robert Andrew Parker encounters his topics daily and through a multitude of circumstances. In 1955 he did the drawings for the film *Lust for Life*, climaxing in a strong identification with van Gogh and his life, his time, and his world. This example represents a deep-felt compassion for van Gogh the artist and driven man.

From a technical point of view, Mr. Parker is not interested in observing any set formula. It may be said that he solves the task with what is on hand at any given moment. In this example two papers are seen to be joined, to enlarge the sheet. The manipulation of tool and medium are simple, direct, and essential. The visual effects employed by Mr. Parker are not the result of artifice. Commenting on this point, he says, "The look of being wiped etc. in the picture is done with a brush and watercolors—no turpentine or other materials. But the paper is comparatively smooth, so I suppose that accounts for some of that appearance."

ROBERT ANDREW PARKER, West Branch #2

This small piece of landscape, no more than a fragment of sky and earth, is powerful in its comprehensive imagery and directness of statement. Simple and elementary forms are balanced in a fusion of bold brush work and color. Sun and roadway come into a magnificent meeting which transcends place and detail. Here the stroke of the brush carries more than itself: it carries living suggestion of the objects it represents.

Color Plates

GEORGE ZORETICH, Landscape

In the painting *Landscape*, the primary intention was to deal with atmospheric relationships. The painting surface—composition board covered with unbleached muslin and Chinese paper—was one that would allow for such intention. The cloth and paper were glued to the board with wheat paste. Transparent watercolor and acrylic were combined in the painting. The paper was first stained with transparent watercolor. Brushes and paint rollers were used to lay in the washes. The rollers were of the kind used in interior house painting—wool, three inches wide. As the painting progressed and initial subtleties gave way to more exact and solid areas—such as the grasses, under-brush, and earth—semi-opaque acrylic was introduced. The acrylic was applied with roller and brush.

In the development of this painting and in others it became apparent that transparent watercolor and acrylic were quite compatible. The absorbent nature of the cloth and paper pulled in and muted the transparent watercolor in numerous instances. In turn, the acrylic allowed for the building up of certain densities more difficult to obtain with transparent watercolor.

CHEN CHI, Man on a Tightrope

From start to finish, this fine work was built-up by the only kind of wash possible with rice paper. Large areas were washed-in by depositing pigment with big enough loads of water to result in its spreading. Placed closely enough, and loaded evenly, each stroke merges with others. Color transitions in this type of wash take on a dappled and softened-off appearance. The conventional wash is impossible on rice paper. Noting other technical information, the paper was mounted as described in the section on stretching, the paint was tube colors, and the brushes preferred by Mr. Chen are pointed sables.

YAR CHOMICKY, Winter Mists

In this example the principle of washing away parts of painted layers was employed. Several rinsings were involved and, after each, sections were detailed further through various wet, moist, and dry stages. Water was permitted free play with pigment and some touchings of pen and ink. The broken wash of the background resulted from not clearing the area of superfluous water and released pigment and inks. The oiliness of the ink used (CADO) acted as a resist, resulting in an unusual texture.

116

Artist: HOBSON PITTMAN
Title: *Summer Bouquet, 1962*
Medium: Pastel

VINCENT VAN GOGH IN ST REMY

Artist: ROBERT ANDREW PARKER
Title: *Vincent van Gogh in St. Remy*
Medium: Watercolor

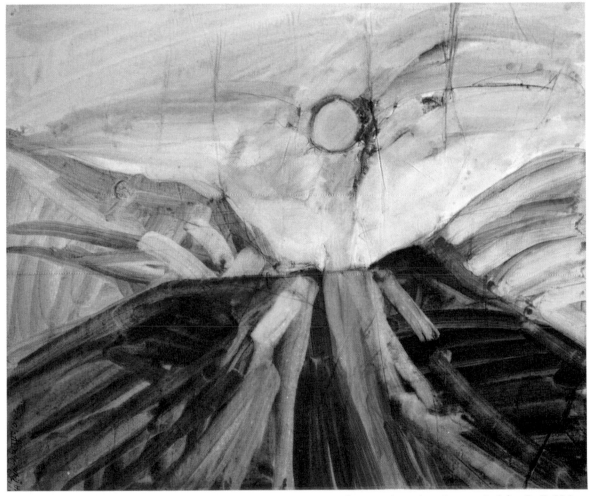

Courtesy the artist; photographed by O. E. Nelson

Artist: *ROBERT ANDREW PARKER*
Title: *West Branch #2*
Medium: Watercolor

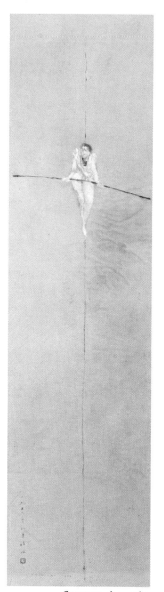

Artist: CHEN CHI
Title: *Man on a Tightrope*
Medium: Watercolor on rice paper

Aritst: GEORGE ZORETICH
Title: *Landscape*
Medium: Transparent watercolor and acrylic

Artist: *YAR CHOMICKY*
Title: *Winter Mists*
Medium: Watercolor and ink

Artist: **ALBERT CHRIST-JANER**

Title: *Sea Forms*

Medium: Polymer tempera

Courtesy the artist

Artist: *BILL HANSON*
Title.   *Ledgemarks*
Medium: Watercolor and pastel

Courtesy the artist

Artist: *BILL HANSON*
Title: *Ledgemarks*
Medium: Watercolor

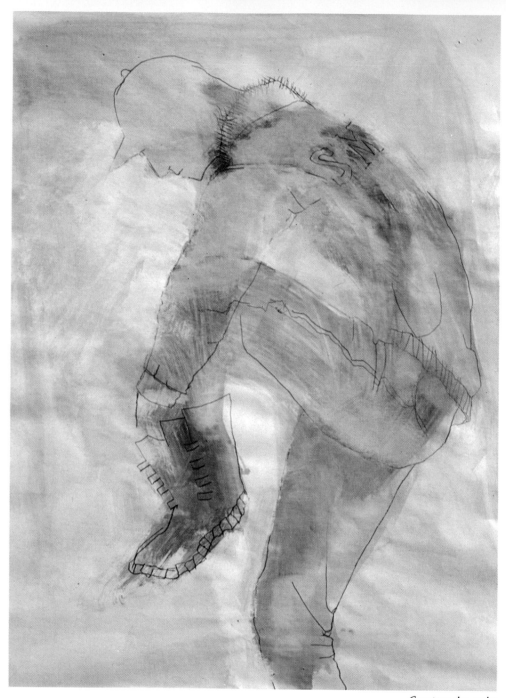

Courtesy the artist

Artist: *STUART FROST*
Title: *Overshoes*
Medium: Gouache and ink

Color Plates

ALBERT CHRIST-JANER, Sea Forms

Innovation and image are inseparable in the works of Albert Christ-Janer. The natural actions or behaviors revealed by the medium establish both technique and topic which, in turn, abstractly suggest earth, sky, and sea. To experience the spirit of his meanings, the artist invites the viewer "to look" and "to contribute your vision to what you see . . . and, in so doing, make it your own discovery."

The procedures developed by artist Christ-Janer favor the working of polymer preparations as fluidly as possible. Painting consists of many floodings of the surface (watercolor paper, rice paper, synthetic "paper") with color and water, supplemented by sprinklings of sand or gravel. These adhere easily with the polymer glues which bind the pigments. For additional tactile and visual variation, overlays of other materials are often introduced or, at some later point, areas may be modified by rinsing with water or solvents and by mechanical means, such as scraping. In describing his approach, Albert Christ-Janer regards his paintings to have been "grown" rather than evolved through traditional process or sequences.

BILL HANSON, Ledgemarks

A favorite picnic spot on Schoodic Point; the red and orange granite ledge, wetted by fresh water winding its way down the long slant to the sea. A tackle box full of watercolor; a portably small sheet of paper. As a photographer I had recorded this spot close-up, using a view camera. The black and white prints revealed what appeared to be an air view of a mighty river. Color photographs revealed a rich surface which might well have been an abstract cave painting done by a contemporary artist—a transformation of time and place.

The camera had simultaneously told the evoked truth of art as well as the plain truth of science. Now, as a painter, I faced the same subject. This time the cues for action came from the unconscious via the brush and the nature of watercolor; a few strokes and a painting emerged—poised in white space. It was a watercolor—abstracted to delicate glazes; a symbol, not a *thing*, not the *place*.

Another approach seemed justified. What of the textural richness and solidity of the granite? What of the mood of *thing* and *place* rather than of surface calligraphy?

This time I used the watercolors with the idea of adding to the work with soft pastel. Combined with watercolor, the pastel would allow an equivalent of the scumble technique in oil. It also would allow for

Color Plates

a second type of white: as well as the untouched white of the paper, I could add opaque white pastel.

The opaque colors of pastel have their own freshness. On rough paper, soft pastel sticks leave a texture-line, similar to dry brush technique.

In short, one can work to attain richness and solidity—another mood, different from the transparent watercolor. In my opinion, this is the validity of mixed media—it makes possible the attaining of a new mood. In this instance, the resulting painting would have been impossible within the limits of watercolor along. Here extended "over-painting" became a counterpoint of good, fresh watercolor technique and good, fresh pastel technique.

With the aid of several media, the artist can prime and enlarge the areas of focused unconscious response to the world. He can work in these several ways to see more of self and more of place.

—Bill Hanson, 1965

STUART FROST, Overshoes

A familiar human action gives meaning to figure painting. Done in a combination of opaque and thinned out overlays, with line definitions in ink of several colors, the whole is compatibly merged. Each medium complements the other, with no visual disruptions.

Artist: *WINSLOW HOMER*
Title: *Woodman and Fallen Tree*
Medium: Watercolor

Man in relation to natural forces was a consuming motive for much of Homer's work. He loved, respected, and lived by the landscape. In this single example almost every quality emphasized in the classic American watercolor tradition is present. The degree of Homer's technical influence should be obvious.

Courtesy Dr. Susan Novikoff

Artist: **MORRIS GRAVES**
Title: *Two Birds*
Medium: Ink wash

"I believe, Morris Graves—with extreme economy of means, for there is not a single superfluous brush stroke in this work—has captured the essence of loneliness in its two fundamental expressions: self-contained sorrow and anguished outcry. I am not sure about Graves' original intentions, but to me the blue ink-wash area which envelops the birds and at the same time separates them from the outer white area, is their 'environment' which affects them—or us—and to which, they—or we—react. The anguished cry of the second bird does not reach with its lament beyond the limits of this 'environment' and the beak of the first bird, carrying the weight of its sorrow in a downward bend, runs parallel to the contour line of this bluish area. The blue itself varies greatly in hue, from a somber darker shade in the birds to a delicate lighter grayish-blue at the outskirts of this surrounding area."
—Dr. Susan Novikoff

painted works. When any did occur, the statement was primitive and stylized, but in the fifteenth century somewhat carefully studied, albeit fanciful and decorative, landscape passages began to appear with greater regularity. Attention to depiction of environment increased even more with the formulation of the laws of perspective and systems of three-dimensional illusions. It was during this time of discovery and new activity that gum-tempered watercolors joined egg tempera as a medium. The aerial quality of transparent watercolor lent itself early to landscape.

In the sixteenth century another spatial dimension was realized. Notions of movement and a sensation of flow and pulsation were infused through baroque ideals. With the seventeenth century and Nicholas Poussin, the landscape model became cast as a setting within which some action takes place. Today the landscape is essentially a problem of depiction of some aspect of nature or surroundings and space which elicits a response and the urge to express it significantly.

The landscape is an inexhaustible pictorial source. In scale, its topic may center upon some feature immediately underfoot, or it may extend into great sweeps of land, water, sky, and infinity. In further contrast with the still life and the figure study, the landscape is not static. Time and objects cannot be immobilized, nor can conditions of change—in light, for example—be controlled. Movements and motions cannot be arrested. The leaf continues to quiver after the first look, and the winds continue to push the cloud to the last horizon, dragging shadows across the valley floor, the mountain, and the seas.

The other senses augment the eye in the experience of landscape. Sound, smell, and touch aid in the description of what the eye detects. Who can look out a window without also "seeing" that it is warm or cold outside? And when the skies blacken with roiling clouds, who doesn't hear the rumbling of thunder somewhere behind the silence of the deep wood and the crows flocking across the snows? The whole body feels the sun's warmth and the chilling wind; the fingers feel bark and rock, the feet the crunch of leaf and twig, the wet of rain, and the grain and frit of sandy shores where gulls shriek.

The landscape is the most complex artistic problem—which makes it all the more worthwhile. It consists of timelessness, of moments and split moments, and of endless relationships of cause and effect. Any instant, any place, and any condition in simultaneous occurrence can be a topic among many. As wanderer and creature of his environment, the landscapist accumulates a store of responses and information. Everything can be of consequence, however small, particularly if it is part of a discovery of life in some form. Rules of spatial representation and their arbitrary demonstration truly lessen in importance when this happens. Surely no exercise can be of as much value as the discovery of living things where none are expected— in the pond, the sand, and under the deep snow where curled, brown ferns arch over glisteningly green and alive teaberry. The cultivation of an intensity of feeling toward the land is a far more vital consciousness than any of the artifices by which space is simulated. Nature is a greater perpetrator of the wayward and accidental than she is a conformist to aesthetic edicts. Taking this as a cue, more direct and spontaneous reaction to a site and less restriction of interpretation become possible.

Watercolor as a painting medium has individual properties and peculiarities that can give the artist concern as well as moments of satisfaction and confidence. Unknowingly one can become satisfied with superficial results all too easily; knowingly, the artist can direct watercolor's fluid quality and fast-changing pace toward subtle complexities that will allow for unusual form and space relationships.

When one is dealing with landscape interpretation and visualization, the possibility of quick and subtle notation can give the experienced painter rich and imaginative excursions into nature and environment. In the same painting the numerous probes may add up to a lyrical orchestration of nature. Needless to say, there are dangers and rewards that can come from such an abundance of variables. The success of the outcome depends upon the artist's ability to recognize the moment of creative decision.

landscape classes

Local setting has given rise to separate terms within the broader landscape definition. In the restricted sense, *landscape* refers primarily to works which emphasize topography. Topics related to

Artist: *JOHN MARIN*
Title: *Ramapo Mountains #5, 1950*
Medium: Watercolor

Nature moves swiftly, spontaneously, unwaiting. The painter must yield to nature's pace; he must utilize his means quickly and with meaningful economy. This landscape is like a moment arrested, stilled in its energy and continuous motion. Here wetness and color spread are where they are because of chance play. Technique follows the facts of action taken in this pure landscape.

the sea are called *seascapes, marine scapes*, or *marines*; depictions of cities are often called *cityscapes*. In some instances the term *sky-scape* occurs, for obvious reasons. The term *pure landscape* refers to works which avoid the inclusion of any manmade objects, such as utility poles, rail fences, and the like. Incidentally, this may be as good a place as any to remind you to refrain from depending upon poles, posts, fences, and wires as convenient ways of tying together any and all compositions!

landscape elements

The landscape consists of topography, vegetation, sky, waters, and manmade structures. Within each as a division, some rather universal observations are possible. Light source, clouds, trees, and other components can be inspected at random and generalizations made.

Topographical features should be understood by the landscapist. A mountain, for instance, must not be simply a drawn line which marks where sky may begin, with another line vaguely establishing its base. Rock, massiveness, thrust, erosion, and sheerness or undulation, depending upon its age and where it is, are some attributes which might better denote a mountain. Bare outline without substance within is insipid; the silhouette most fitting to any object is that which is organic to it, a result of structural fact. This is true of the mountain, and it is just as true of clods of dirt overgrown with wild grass and daisies in a fallow field.

In the lowland and valley, streams cut through ravines and meadows. Winds are steady, kites dip in the skies, and the plow breaks the ground into ridges of black, moist, and fragrant chunks of earth. A patchwork quilt of acres of tossing wheat, rising corn, Queen Anne's lace, tiger lily, cornflower, and blackberry vines at some places; elsewhere asphalt and concrete, white-lined into parking stalls, are packed down into a last sterile stratum. The new landscape! Where the wild flower grew, billboards have sprouted, trees have fallen, and dirt and litter fly where milkweed is no more. Here blight is architect and junkyards the major industry—on a par with strip mines, steel mills, quarries, and drive-in theaters, hot-dog stands, and shopping centers. And overhead the cables and high voltage lines hang heavier and heavier, bending poles and cutting off views, but delivering improved television images and clearer and faster communication. How long will it be before the earth itself will be completely wrapped with lead and copper, like a ball of twine made by some frugal saver of string? Before the megalopolis is complete, the classical landscape will remain awhile longer, for the sentimental or, in the jargon of the day, the square. Meanwhile, the hip can look forward to more neon, incandescence, fluorescence, and the campiest of way-out inspirational sources.

VEGETATION

The painter need not be a botanist, but if he is alert he notices how plants grow. He may not know species by name, but he recognizes their differences, their physical and seasonal appearances, and the effects upon them through natural actions such as sun, wind, rain, and snow.

Trees are to be found everywhere, and therefore particular attention will be given them. Rather than offer recipes for the painting of trees, I shall remark upon them broadly, in the hope that this may be more helpful in the end. Details may be studied in one's own way and as needed for more clarification. The inclusion of every detail observed does not necessarily make for better depiction, whether the object is a tree or anything else. Simplifying complex forms rather than elaborating them is in keeping with enjoyable design and the demands of the medium.

Much about the landscape can be learned if time is taken to observe action and change in the landscape over a prolonged period, as over the span of a year for example. Just as occasionally "the tree cannot be seen for the forest," so also it cannot be known without looking for the effects of natural forces on it. Taking the winter months for a start, the structures of land and plant life can be readily studied. The orders and aberrations of natural growth are more evident then. The shape of trees, their proportion and relationship of parts, their colors and the distortions they have undergone are more clearly and dramatically revealed. The straight tree, the perfect-

Artist: *CHARLES BURCHFIELD*
Title: *East Wind and Winter Sun*
Medium: Watercolor

With expressionist license, the sky is pure invention. Observable fact is of less reality than form and movement shaped by the wind. The mood of a March day can be felt. Swirls of light echoed by the dark move briskly through space and along the ground, like quicksilver. And the sun hangs quietly, behind a veiling of cloud.

Noteworthy, too, is the contradiction of styles. Sky and ground are not consistent with each other in concept. There is no reason why this should not be, unless one cares to insist on visual agreement for its own sake.

ly bisymmetric and faultlessly branched tree is a myth. Trees lean at an angle from having been turned by prevailing winds. Branches twist into heavier massings on the downwind side for the same reason. Twining comes also from following the sun's path. Seen against backgrounds of snow, these features of trees are definite, suggesting calligraphic qualities.

Winter or not, trees are always full of color. Intensity may change seasonally, but there is color all the same. The willow's branches are tinged with ochre and sienna through the winter, and brighten more with the first rains of spring. Alizarin and gray, dark greenish blacks, and light blues etch the woodlands in line and blurrings in the cold months. Light hazes of red and purple appear before buds begin to open into fresh greens and blossoms. Trees of summer hold green until fall's spectacular color changes introduce gaudy reds, yellows, and purples, except in dry years when foliage goes from green to brown. When winter comes, again the empty nests are seen, and the last brown leaves of some types of oak hang on, to drop when loosened by April rains.

What may be observed of trees may be applied also to other vegetative life, of course. A point to remember, however, is that there must be agreement of details in a painting. A maple tree ablaze with yellow could not be correct, for example, if a crocus, too, is in bloom. Rocks tumbled by the sea and granite formations could not appear next to a Kansas wheat field. And a cattail next to a starfish? Whatever the place, pay attention to its character and naturalness of details.

THE SKY

In the realm of watercolor painting the sky as a graduated wash often seems to be the extent of any discussion. Broken coloration, overcasts, cloud formations, and common meteorological conditions are scarcely mentioned. Those who are interested in landscape painting, surely, should equip themselves with information beyond the average.

Atmospheric dusts, the position of the sun as a source of light, and the season of the year affect the sky's color. Its local color is blue, on the warm side during temperate months and icily cold during the winter. When the sun is close to the horizon, vibrant yellows and reds flood the sky, notably at sunset, as atmospheric dust and water vapor refract light, producing a vibrant glow—a sign of clear weather ahead to farmer and mariner. In the eastern skies, meanwhile, shadows thicken and colors deepen, with only the rising moon to cast a pearl's light. Waning day and coming night have appeared together in the same painting from time to time. Night, ever intriguing, is an often neglected possibility.

Clouds are occasionally overlooked, at least in their identification. The universal cloud, if this is possible, is a pretension of the cumulus class; a fair weather cloud, its popularity may be associated with the notion that painting by and large is a fair weather activity. Faked sky and cloud relationships, however, can be greatly disappointing. Real knowledge of clouds is essential to convey accuracy and mood in any landscape.

In dealing with lighting in the landscape, consideration of the various angles of the sun from one hour to the next is of primary importance. The color of clouds at sunset, in fact, is partly due to the sun's position. The direction and length of shadows also depend upon the direction from which light comes. And in planning a composition, it must be determined how the setting is stationed in respect to the light source. Shall sidelighting be selected? Would the idea be developed to greater advantage if front lighting were favored? Or might not backlighting be a better scheme? And what would happen if the work were oriented to lighting from immediately above? In raising the question, some answers are implied. A long look at a site under each condition might be of real value.

Where there is direct light, there is reflected light also. Some materials absorb light rays, others reflect them. Without reflected lighting, shadows would be colorless and dull, lifeless and flat. Complete absence of a feeling of light anywhere in a watercolor is a disaster contrary to the characteristic sparkle of the medium, and shadowed areas are particularly vulnerable to this failing. Blue is a frequent color used to suggest shadows, as is purple. The complementary hue to the local color of the area to be shadowed is another workable suggestion. But perhaps just as satisfactory results might be obtained if shadowed areas were infused with hints of color which

Artist: ADOLF DEHN
Title: Lake George, 1957
Medium: Watercolor

Tranquility and a glorious light pervade this landscape interpretation by one of the most significant watercolorists in American art. The splendor of sun, cloud, and sky are magnificently understood and conceived. There is no area in this work which is not a deeply sensed, living experience. The handling of the medium is adjusted to the subject, down to the last nuance.

might be reflected from surrounding objects, which are illuminated themselves.

The reflection of light on water as well as the reflections of objects pose minor problems of physics. Some generalizations may prove helpful in place of complicated explanations. Factors of reflection

Artist: *MORRIS GRAVES*
Title: *Spring With Machine Age Noise #1*
Medium: Tempera, ink

     The pure landscape is no more, the machine intrudes. Cutting blades mow and chew everything in their path, scourging all that is natural and driving out all life with a clatter. No birds singing in the moonlight here. But soon the bells of the Good Humor man will sound.

are governed by the *angle of incidence* of light. A perfectly smooth mirroring surface reflects a reverse image of objects in such a way that they appear to be as far behind the surface as they are, in fact, in front of it. Light rays travel in a straight line; when reflected, they travel also in a straight line in the opposite direction but at the same angle at which they entered. These angles are the angle of incidence and the angle of reflection. A quiet body of water reflects images with little distortion, but if disturbed by the wind, images are broken and only light is reflected. The dancing glitters of light on the surface of large bodies of water are the dispersed image of the sun—that is, they are a composite of innumerable reflections of the sun. These images also result in secondary reflections of the first reflection. This is happening whenever reflected light on water appears elongated, from the position of the light to the spot at which the viewer stands. Where there is more than one light source, the reflections of each converge upon the viewer from several directions at once, like long bands across the water.

For pictorial representation, some reminders may prove helpful. The reverse image of reflections means, in short, that everything is upside-down. Reflections of trees at the edge of water will be of the underside, as when one looks upward at an actual tree. The under parts of clouds are seen in reflection. The underside of a building's eaves is seen, but the roof is not. As objects recede toward the horizon, they cannot be seen in reflection. Perpendicular objects are reflected in the perpendicular; where other angles are involved, the reflection will be in reverse at an equal angle. The tilt of a tree, for example, appears reversed on water.

The color values of reflected lights and objects are slightly modified from the original. Lighter values are dropped in register, and shadowed areas are raised. These are small adjustments, but they are effective.

MARINE PAINTING

Coastal regions attract painters and would-be painters in droves each summer. At no other time of the year is the production ratio of inferior works to quality art higher. Vacationing amateurs give the setting a try, for new experience and relaxation. On this count they deserve some indulgence. On the other hand, bad art is encouraged and hawked at every turn as souvenirs and mementoes of a pleasurable stay.

The images associated with places next to the sea are usually overpopularized details. For years the innocent have painted the identical things and in almost identical ways. In one New England village the center of interest is a lobster shack, forever enshrined as the symbol, first and last, of nautical romanticism. Neatly painted, with red and white floats and netting artfully hung on one wall, this small building stands in the open on a granite quay and is called *Motif No. 1*. In the same harbor there are rocks, not yet rearranged. And in the water, submerged green and yellow islands of seaweed nod and sway in the currents.

In the same locality typical villages are to be found where life is unaffected. These are the homes of the fishing fleets, of the men

Artist: *JOHN MARIN*
Title: *Region of Brooklyn Bridge Fantasy, 1932*
Medium: Watercolor

Juxtaposition of forms into out-of-plane relationships results in a composite of independent spatial illusions in this presentation of an urban place. Multiple images overlay one another, formal perspective is destroyed, and the single setting is fractured into kaleidoscopic bits and pieces. Sun, brick, mortar, height, distance, air, sound, sky, and cloud—all are here.

Artist: *JOHN MARIN*
Title: *Sea Piece*
Medium: Watercolor

 With a spontaneous and natural hand, John Marin characteristically reduced images to their essential substance. The force of wave and the movement of sun and time are unmistakable. The medium, too, is set into motion and left to its own spontaneous devices. Here is the sea, eternal and ceaseless. From a technical viewpoint, the drawing traits resemble the qualities produced by quill points, broad pens, and, in particular, the dropper attached to the cap of India ink bottles.

Artist: *LYONEL FEININGER*
Title: *A Walk Along The Shore, 1940*
Medium: Watercolor

     For those accustomed to the geometric stylizations for which he is known, this fantasy-like interpretation by Lyonel Feininger may come as a surprise. Yet the mood of space and light of his other works is here, too. The strange forms in the center hover near the horizon, much like his sailing ships elsewhere. The grouping of figures, done in almost a childlike way, are reminiscent of figures at the edge of seas and strong shaftings of light in better known compositions.

of the Outer Banks, where life is not glamorized. Also along the same coast are lonely beaches and ocean sounds, marshes and ponds. Perhaps the greatest difficulty of painting in the vicinity of the sea is the finding of topic which has not been exploited and reduced to the "picturesque."

CHAPTER 5

On Papers

Normally, beginning students will be content to execute their paintings on papers of average quality. Advanced students, practiced amateurs, and professional painters will, however, desire papers with more exceptional characteristics.

Selection of watercolor papers is best determined after having tried and experienced their various characteristics. Preferences are the result of individual painting requirements, for purposes of effect and even tactile satisfactions. To aid selection, paper surfaces are classified with these standard designations according to attributes:

Hot-pressed (HP) is extremely smooth. It lends itself to detailed indications and, in general, might be considered most suitable for representational styles.

Artist: *KARL SCHRAG*
Title: *The Island*
Medium: Watercolor, ink, crayon on rice paper

There is a shimmering and floating quality imparted by this work on rice paper. Hard pointed tools, crayon and pen in this example, will tear rice paper if not used with care. Not having any tooth itself, rice paper gets a semblance of tooth from surfaces underneath it, in a manner similar to the taking of a rubbing. The work is conceived in drawing terms.

Cold-pressed (CP) is medium in texture, neither smooth nor rough. It is the most popular of surfaces and satisfies a broad range of technical needs.

Rough (R) is the most pronounced tooth. It is least sympathetic to detailed work, yet for sparkling, crisp, and broken passages it is most gratifying.

Water on paper causes the sheet to expand by swelling its fibers. Buckling—"hills and valleys"—distorts the work plane, limiting manipulations and creating dissatisfaction. Even the seemingly negligible amount of water contacting the paper's surface as a painting progresses is sufficient to bring about the onset of this distressing condition. What occurs is an erratic combination of tensions resulting from wet and dry areas affecting the body of the paper support. The weight or thickness of paper is important in this respect, for the amount of cockle is directly related to the weight of a paper and may be minimized by selecting the heavier varieties. Papers of 140 pounds are recommended as a minimum weight for most purposes, although 70 and 90 pound papers are manageable. Heavier papers also have the advantage of being able to bear harsh and severe treatment— scraping with sharp tools, for example—without being damaged.

A third important factor in considering papers is the quality of their fiber compositions. The finest of paper is that manufactured from linen rags. These are carefully produced by hand and great attention is paid to the elimination of impurities, such as metal particles, and to the neutralizing of bleaching agents which might become activated later and affect a painting adversely. These papers are also carefully and properly sized specifically for watercolor purposes. A quality paper is easily recognized by the manufacturer's embossed or watermarked symbols. This signature usually indicates the side intended as the working ground, since not all papers are finished on both sides. Usually the reverse side carries flaws, blemishes, and other irregularities which may be disconcerting. American machine-made papers are of quality appropriate to meet good watercolor standards for exploratory and warm-up sessions.

RICE PAPER

Rice paper stems back to the very beginnings of the history of papermaking. In fiber content and mode of manufacture, there is little difference between modern rice papers and the earliest specimens produced in China in the year 105, during the reign of Emperor Ho. Credited with having invented the process is Ts'ai Lung, a court official.

The first papers appear to have been made of bark fibers, hemp fibers, and old fishnets. The bark fiber was taken from a particular species of mulberry—not the same as that upon which silkworms were fed, however. Other fibers have been used since to develop papers for sundry uses and to make use of regional vegetable fibers— straw and bamboo among them.

Most of the rice paper available today comes from Japan, although other specimens are produced throughout the Far East in lesser quantity. The most frequent fibers used are *gampi, kozo,* and *mitsumata.* They occupy the top of the paper hierarchy, and each represents classic qualities. *Gampi* is noble and dignified; it is made from the *gampi,* a plant which once grew wild in the mountain near Shuzenji Temple at Shuzenji in the province of Sagami. The sturdiest, *kozo,* is regarded as masculine and strong. Its sinewy, tough fibers come from the *kozo* tree, a member of the mulberry family. *Mitsumata,* a brownish paper, is made from a cultivated plant bearing the same name. Of the three, *kozo* is the most important as an artist's paper because of durability.

Much rice paper continues to be handmade. The process has changed little, if at all, either from the original or from that learned by the Arabs after they captured the city of Samarkand from the Chinese, about 704 A.D. The Arabs began to manufacture paper when they returned to their own towns and cities. Another war, the Crusades, introduced paper manufacture into Europe.

The primitive process of preparing paper is quite simple. In China and in Japan this ancient method is still popular and an important part of the economy as farmers in both countries employ themselves during the winter months with home manufacture of paper. The method described here follows the Chinese method.

Mulberry branches are boiled in lye, to remove the bark. After several days of maceration in water, the inner bark is scraped from the outer part and boiled in lye until it separates into fibers. Washed in a pan or sieve, the fibers are worked by hand into a pulp, which is then spread on a table and beaten fine with a mallet. Placed in a tub containing a "soup" consisting of rice and *oveni* root, these and the pulp are thoroughly stirred into a mixture. *Oveni* and rice are mucilagenous materials. Sheets are formed by dipping a wooden

Artist: *ANDREE RUELLAN*
Title: *Ravines #2*
Medium: Watercolor on rice paper

Rice papers impart a fragility to a work as no other paper can. And, in its own way, it will support crispness and even, if need be, large, bold strokes. Something of the extent to which manipulations can go appears to be explored in this brush drawing.

frame fitted with a "mold," or screen, as a bottom into a vat of pulp. A thin layer of pulp collects on the screen when the frame is lifted away. The sheets are stacked as they are made with strips of reeds placed between them. They are placed under a load of weights and left to dry in the sun. A typical screen is made of slender reeds, or of thin splinters of bamboo, which are tied together with fine threads. Lacquered silk gauge is sometimes used as a screen.

Like other handmade papers, rice papers come in single sheets. Machine-made rice papers, on the other hand, are sold in roll lengths. Each roll consists of a given number of sheets which are mechanically joined by overlapped ends. Each sheet is cut away from the roll at each juncture when it is to be used. One attractive feature of hand-made rice paper is that it is available in sizes as large as 28 inches by 68 inches.

painting characteristics of rice papers
Rice papers wet very quickly, and this fact should be realized early. Absorbent when used by itself, and even more so and for longer duration when mounted over cloth, this characteristic must be used to advantage or it will defeat the painter.

If a fairly dry ground is maintained, painting on rice paper can proceed from simple, direct, and economical brushwork to more complex and technically involved build-ups of color and effects. What dryness can do and what wetness can do—these are properties to be learned.

As mentioned in another part of this volume, wet-on-wet approaches should not be attempted with rice paper where there is high saturation of water. Complete paintings can literally dissolve if done on a wet surface. Curiously enough, wetting rice paper on which a painting has dried completely will not disturb it. If wetted gently when not quite dry, some beautifully softened areas result. In this instance, bathing the entire painting—even under the fine spray of a garden hose—will wash off unset pigment. When it has dried after each rinsing, the painting can be carried further, progressing in essentially wet-on-dry conditions.

In the accompanying photographic series some features of rice paper are identified. No effort to complete the demonstration into a painting is intended.

Rice paper has one smooth and hard side, one soft and fuzzy side. Mount the hard side face up if brush style is to be hard-edged, face down for essentially diffused effects. Permit rice mountings to dry completely. The customary wet-in-wet approach is impossible with rice papers.

1. This painting has been left unfinished for several weeks. It is now dry and ready for any new effects that may come to mind. Here some dark spottings and deeper wash shapes have been added. The middle value strokes have not affected lines and areas painted earlier.

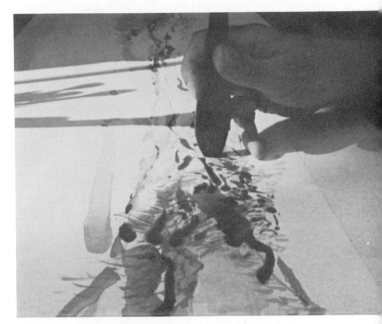

2. For no other reason than to demonstrate a change of tool, some ink markings are included. A deep value is thereby established. Note that it holds its position.

3. Inking is continued into another part of the work.

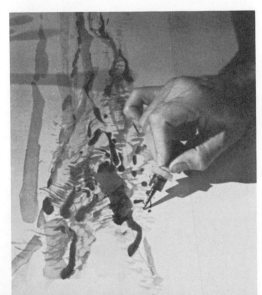

4. Some "softening-off" is tried where ink has been placed a few moments earlier.

5. In the lower corner the tip of a flat brush begins to leave a series of markings. The brush is at full load, carrying watercolor. Each touching is held for several seconds without reloading. Each time enough water is imbibed to cause spreading.

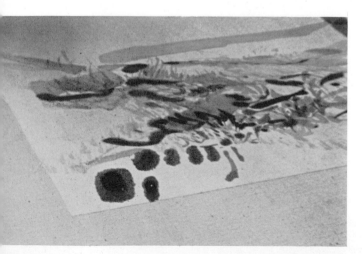

6. The indications in the corner continue to enlarge and spread, revealing the blotting power of the paper.

7. Clear water is laid over the work that has been done thus far. The water causes "softening-off" of the last markings, but other painted portions are not affected.

8. With a pointed brush, some darks are added. This part of the panel is in a wet-in-wet state which should not be continued for long. The darkened area comes of a toned all-over wash which has crept beyond the edge of the paper into the area of the muslin and is spreading in other directions as well—toward the center and the top of the paper.

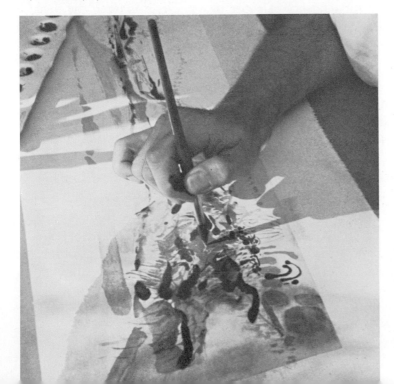

CUSTOM-MADE PAPERS

Occasionally papers with off-standard characteristics are desirable. In such cases papers can be produced to embody special characteristics of size, thickness, content; and working attributes can be incorporated as specified. An expert can, for instance, fabricate a paper which is required to dry within a prescribed time limit and to behave in other unique ways which foster effects preferred by the painter.

Many artists of Japan, and an increasing number in the United States, use custom-made papers only, complete with private water marks. Paper houses in Japan provide this service upon request, gladly and economically. In the United States rare individuals can be located who will produce limited quantities more out of love for craftsmanship and quality than for profit.

ON STRETCHING

Because of the tendency of paper to wrinkle, it is often the practice to mount, or stretch, the paper by one of several means. As noted elsewhere, this characteristic is most apparent in the lighter weights of paper (72 pounds or less). Demands of time, economy, and the size of the paper are other factors relevant to the purposes for stretching and the method elected.

The heavy weight grades, 250 to 400 pounds, have the advantage of not requiring a stretch of any kind. If fastened down at all, they may be simply tacked to a drawing board or like support. Papers already mounted to heavy cardboard—illustration board type—are already stretched, thinner papers. Another exception to the need for stretching is paper which is marketed in block form, similar to a tablet but bound along all sides; this paper, however, is not free from buckling and is satisfactory only with limited amounts of moistening. Fastening light and intermediate weight paper, while dry, with masking tape to a board is successful if here, too, little water saturation is anticipated. Wet techniques are likely to be more controllable if the sheets, exclusive of the heaviest grades, of course, are stretched. Some optional stretching practices are suggested below.

Soak paper in a large sink or tub, allowing it to swell, and calculate the interval of immersion according to its weight. The time will be a matter of only several minutes. As a rule-of-thumb the time of wetting may be gauged according to the amount of water any single panel is expected to absorb after a painting has been begun. Shake off excess moisture and fit to an open frame, such as canvas stretchers of the type used in oil painting. With the edges creased and lapped over the sides of the frame, the paper is gently pulled, starting at the middle of each side and outward toward the corners, and tacked as one proceeds. Upon drying, the surface will be taut and resilient. Caution is advised against too tight a stretch, as ripping may occur or the frame may be warped out of plane in withstanding the tensions of the drying paper. This method is particularly advantageous for wet-in-wet techniques, because the painting may be kept continuously moist by applying additional water from behind as desired. Panels of this design are light in weight. They are ideal for carrying on sketching jaunts. To take further advantage of this fact, stretch a second painting paper on the reverse side of the frame.

When the paper has been wetted as above, it may be fastened more simply with gummed tape to a drawing board, masonite, or any similar hard surface in lieu of stretchers. The resiliency of unbacked paper will be absent, but one may prefer an unyielding painting ground while at the same time gaining in expediency. Paper stretched in this way may sometimes require that another sheet, often of common wrapping paper, be affixed to the reverse side to counteract any likelihood of warping of the support, which happens when the backing board is too thin for the paper size. This technique is like counter-enameling metal in enameling processes. The necessity for such backing may be exploited by mounting a sheet of watercolor paper on each side of the board, thereby stretching two workable papers, as in the case of open frames. However, with this method, the paper may split if it has been oversoaked.

Still another procedure is to sponge both sides of a paper, followed by a smooth brushing of one side with an application of library paste or vegetable glue. The sheet this time is adhered to a heavy cardboard by pressing down with a brayer or roller. Protect the surface with a clean covering of paper. The reverse side of the cardboard should be reinforced with another paper sheet for the reasons already explained. Under no circumstances should rubber-type adhesives be used, as they deteriorate rapidly and do not allow wetted papers to expand properly.

While not all agree to the worth of the stretching of papers, the process does freshen and cleanse away soil and dirt acquired during storage.

stretching conventional papers   The most common and simple method of stretching paper is easily mastered. It consists of wetting the paper and taping it to a rigid panel.

In preparation, have available pre-cut strips of gummed paper tape within easy reach. Saturate the paper with water by soaking or, as shown here, by liberally squeezing water from a sponge. Do this to both sides. Avoid vigorous rubbing of the paper's surface. Place the paper on its support, in a horizontal elevation, and lightly sponge and lift away excess water, working outward from the center. Turn the paper over and repeat the last step. While reversing the paper, wipe away excess water from the masonite panel.

With the paper positioned as intended, wet the pieces of tape, singly, overlapping each along the edges of the paper and the panel. Smooth the tape with even pressure. Allow the paper to dry; although the ensuing locking of both the paper and the tape will not be proof of the success of the operation, have heart. With shrinkage, the paper will tighten into its original flatness, tautly held by the tapes.

When stretching, prepare a number of panels—ten or more—as interruptions while painting for the sake of stretching additional panels can throw a painter off stride. Actually, the making of panels is time-consuming, mechanical, and even tedious, which, for some is reason enough to restrict this necessity to time allotted beforehand, just to get it over with. A full evening is time well-spent for stretching purposes; daylight hours should be conserved. Brushes, tools, pigments, and the like can be checked for the following day's work.

CONVENTIONAL STRETCHING

1.   A sheet of paper is liberally sponged with water on both sides. The water is allowed to flow and to be imbibed by the paper without scrubbing or too heavy a hand at any time. To evenly distribute the wetting, take up excessive moisture from one side and then the other with the sponge, or roll the paper into a tube for a few moments.

2.   The paper has been laid on a mount and the taping down of its edges has been begun. Gummed paper tape, at least two inches in width, is suitable for most weights of paper. Here the tape is being wetted by means of a sponge. In some ways it is better to run the strips of tape through a bath, fully immersed. This will swell the tape, and there will be less loss of glue than when rubbed by the sponge. In this way, the drying of the tape and the setting of its glue will be retarded; it will slide along with the shrinkage of the paper, taking hold of the paper and the mounting board when tensions of drying have subsided.

3.   The tape is smoothed in place, one edge at a time. When all edges are down, the panel is put aside to dry. If the paper is prone to cockling, it is at this time that this distortion will begin and develop to more or less prominence. To begin painting at this time would be a mistake. Wait at least until the paper shows a matt surface, when the shine of water is gone. Conventional handmade water color papers are mounted usually with the best side up. The watermark—the maker's signature—determines the proper side.

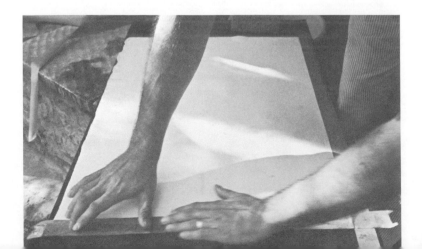

The fragility of rice paper requires a more careful and exacting process to lay it on a backing. The secret, if such a mystery can be said to exist, is in the handling of water itself. The fullest attention must be focused on water application. Also quite necessary is a wide *hake* brush, because of its unique softness and resiliency.

In preparing for rice paper stretching, have on hand sections of muslin a little larger than the size and shape of the paper to be used. If these have been laundered, later shrinking will not be a problem; ironing is not necessary. The crinkles in the fabric when dry are frequently retained, as Chen Chi often does, to give a texture beneath the paper. With the muslin, a thin mixture of wheat (wallpaper) paste and a large brush are needed. A whitewash brush or any large house-painting brush will serve adequately. A large pan of clear water completes the equipment required.

Letting the backing—masonite, Upsom board, plywood, or any thick paper composition board—serve as a momentary table, apply wheat paste to the muslin, turn it over, and even it with a large brush. Allowing the paste to work its way through the weave is desirable, as it will later become the adhesive for the rice paper. Dipping the muslin into the paste bucket and wringing it by hand-twisting is also an expedient way of loading the cloth with paste.

With the muslin ground ready, the trimmed-to-size paper is attached. This is the most critical phase, so an exciting apprehension should enliven the whole business. When hesitations are overcome, raise the rice paper to a hovering distance above the muslin and estimate its placement. Cause the sheet to sag at its middle, then lower this belly into position on the support. To accomplish that which follows, solicit the aid of someone at hand to keep one half of the paper in raised position while you do the same to the other end.

With one hand freed, flood the gutter of the poised paper with water, carrying it along with the *hake* brush. Add more water to brush air bubbles away from the center. The water serves to displace the trapped air, while also providing the paper a cushioning which protects it from the passes of the brush. Superfluous water will be edged aside in the process, to mingle with the water to be applied next.

When the bubbles have been removed, lower more paper slightly at one side of the adhered middle, loading more water and continuing as before. Do this until one of the halves is completely down and no air and water globules appear. Attend to the other half exactly as to the first.

Rice paper absorbs water quickly; consequently, speed and adeptness should be attained sooner or later. The surprising strength of rice papers contributes to successful stretching. As an added reminder, avoid tearing the paper surface by heavy brushing. Maintain a light touch and be certain the *hake* brush is always loaded with water to its capacity.

STRETCHING OF RICE PAPER

Drawings and paintings may be executed on rice papers without being stretched beforehand. When done in this way, the paper will be "wavy" and raised in places. The method described here may be used to lay down paper either before beginning to paint or afterward, to mount the final work. Shown here is the readying of rice paper panels.

1.   Trim papers to their desired sizes and shapes. Have nearby a thinned solution of wheat paste (wallpaper paste), a brush for its application, a container of fresh water, and a soft-haired brush, among the best of which is Japanese *hake*.

2. A piece of muslin, slightly larger than the paper, is pasted to the mounting board. The cloth should be filled with paste. Paste may be applied to both sides by brush, or the cloth may be impregnated by dipping it in the paste, in which case the excess may be removed by wringing it out. Creases in the cloth may be preserved to give an underlying texture to the paper.

3. The cloth is straightened and aligned in respect to the edges of the mounting board. Smoothing may be done by hand, as shown, for the removal of air and paste lumps. There should be an even layer of paste on the surface of the cloth. It will adhere to the rice paper.

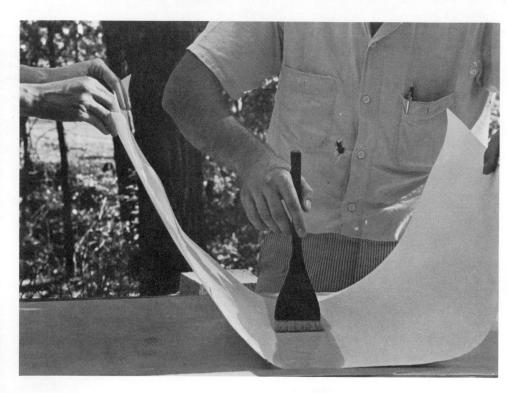

4.   Laying down of the paper is the most critical part. Some assistance may be needed, especially when tried for the first time. Keeping the paper raised, allow it to sag at its middle, then touch it to the paste-covered cloth. With a wide *hake* brush, the resulting trough is flooded with clear water, and lightly moved along.

5.   Some small pockets of air will become trapped between the paper and the cloth. Wetted areas should be flooded with more water which, prodded by the brush, displaces and moves air pockets toward the outer edges of the paper and toward the dry sections of the paper.

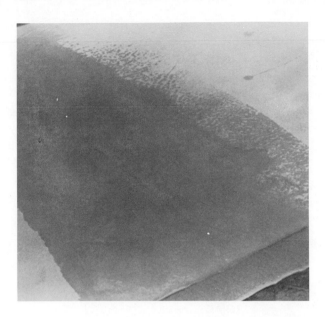

6. For a brief moment the brush is lifted away to show air bubbles. They are seen as the small, rounded, lighter spots. Note the wetness beginning to appear along one edge of the wetted area from the paste beneath the paper.

7. Laying down of the first half is almost completed. Notice the great amount of water held by the brush. Wettings parallel and overlap one another. Some small air bubbles are still in evidence. It is still possible at this point to raise the paper again, in spite of its wetness, and to drive out bubbles by adding more water and repeating the previous steps. There is the risk, however, of breaking the sheet and overstretching it.

8. A large air pocket is shown about to be forced from under the paper. A new load of water, seen as the ridge between the edge of the brush and the air pocket—the light area to which a finger is pointed—has been worked under the paper.

9. The brush shoves the air pocket to the closest corner where it will be forced out.

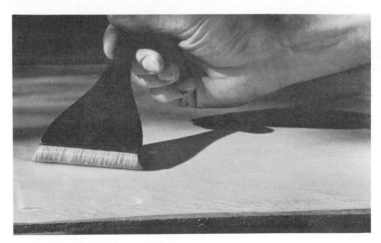

10. With one half of the paper down, the second half is stretched in the same way. When down in full, the mounting is inspected for air bubbles, which are eliminated as described. A renewal of wetting serves to clear the surface of superfluous paste, if any.

ADDENDA ON PAPERS

Watercolor papers are cut into standard sizes. Old designations which once identified the manufacturer's watermark now refer to some sizes. European paper sizes and weights are as follows:

Demy	15½″ × 20″	25 lb.
Medium	17½″ × 22½″	34 lb.
Royal	18″ × 24″	40-60 lb.
Imperial	22½″ × 30½″	70-300 lb.
Double Elephant	26¼″ × 40″	130-250 lb.
Antiquarian	31″ × 53″	240 lb.

Most papers are available in all sizes and weights, but some are more popular than others and the supply may vary. Reliable papers may be selected from among the following brands:

Arches	David Cox
Arnold	Fabriano
A.W.S.	J. Green
Burlington	Michallet
Cartridge	R.W.S.
Creswick	Van Gelder
Crisbrook	Whatman

White Canson

Some papers are toned or tinted. "Camber-sand" has a sand-tone finish. De Wint is gray. David Cox is tinted in three values: Light Rough, Medium Rough, and Dark Rough. Papers in a range of color may also be had, but the tints do not always prove permanent.

Oriental art papers suitable for watercolor:

Hosho	17½	× 23
Hosho Special	25	× 37
Gazen	26	× 54
Toshi	17½	× 27
Kozu (Kozo)	24	× 39
Kozu Art	21	× 29
Kozu Special	21	× 29

Kochi	20	× 26	(20 lb.)
	20	× 26	(44 lb.)
Toyama Art	20	× 26	(26 lb.)
	20	× 26	(48 lb.)
Mochizuki	24	× 26	
Hosokawa	20	× 29	
Hodomura	20	× 26	
	24	× 36	
Mino Buff	23	× 37	

Above groups available through Yasutomo and Co., 24 California Street, San Francisco, California 94111.

Hosho	19	× 24
Hosho Student Grade	16	× 22
Hosho Pure	17½	× 22½
Moriki No. 1009	25	× 36
Mulberry	24	× 33½
Mulberry Student Grade		
Sekishu (white & natural)	24	× 39
Shogun	17½	× 22½
Lightweight		
Heavyweight		
Torinoko	21	× 31

Above recommendation of Andrews-Nelson-Whitehead, 7 Laight Street, New York, N.Y. 10013. Addresses of area outlets available by letter.

SYNTHETIC PAPERS

In recent years laboratory produced "papers" made of cellulose acetate have been introduced for artistic use. They are made to resemble papers in all respects—in appearance, weight, texture, and general behavior. These likenesses are remarkable and found acceptable by most users. The main advantages are the ability to withstand hard handling, cockling, and the more usual effects which water has on paper. Not all watercolor manipulations on such papers or cloths are quite equivalent to the same effects attempted on rag papers. Spreading actions seem to stop sooner and the softening-off of edges is not quite as fluid. There are some effects not obtainable on other grounds. Taking this observation further might lead to some new and interesting optical scales. The material is permanent and guaranteed not to yellow. Users of polymer temperas are discovering it more and more, with great satisfaction.

CHAPTER 6

On Brushes

The brush has been the most prominent tool in
the development and advancement of painting techniques;
that it will ever lose its position of first importance
is quite unlikely. The first function of a brush is to transfer
paint mixtures to the working surfaces. Of course,
this may be accomplished by other means, but no substitute device or action can surpass the brush for
virtuosity and intimacy during the total painting process
itself. Jackson Pollock may have dribbled house-
paint on canvas, but even this important innovator did
not surrender his brushes entirely. In any of its
several forms, the brush is difficult to foresake.

The modern brush has evolved from a lowly reed,
macerated at one end into a clump of shredded fibers, to
a carefully crafted and precise instrument. Other

early improvisations included wool yarn tied to a reed handle and human hair bound with thread to a stick. Out of these humble prototypes the simple fabricating principle for standardization and quantity production was founded. The common brush consists of no more than a tuft of hair fastened to a handle with a ferrule, differing only in materials, styles, and size.

During manufacture of artist-grade brushes, quality controls are fastidious and assembling is exacting. Only the best of animal hairs are prescribed, and operations center on their selection, treatment, and mounting. After being cut, brush hairs are sterilized and mechanically sorted according to length. Placed in a small cylindrical tube, the hairs are shaken into alignment with one another and are pulled by hand into a tuft shape, flag ends outward. The flag ends group into a brush tip naturally, very much as one's own hair "stays down" when uncut for a prolonged period of time; whereas if the butt end of hairs is used, the tip will be spread and stiff. The hairs are gathered together at their butt ends, and trimmed, tied, and dipped into a rubber, pitch, or synthetic adhesive, to make the brush base. This end, the base, is inserted into one opening of the ferrule, usually a metal cylinder, and the handle is inserted into the opposite ferrule opening. Mechanical pressure is then applied to lock tuft and handle into the finished brush. When quill handles are used, as they often are in producing the smallest brushes, twisted rings of wire truss the tuft to the hollow quill.

BRUSH CLASSIFICATION

While there is a technically uniform system of brush classification, it has been obscured by secondary nomenclatures and frequent misnomers. Distinguishing features seem to be responsible for a web of confusing identifications. Type and quality of tuft, its shape, size, and other specialized modifications account for brush groups in themselves. Hair type is the only physical characteristic common to all, however. Categorizing by hair type is the first order of brush classification. Other categories refer to design differences. Reduced to terms of texture, coarse and fine or *hard* and *soft*, two primary groups emerge, which may also be categorized by the animal hairs which are most representative of each. Thus *bristle* and *sable* come to be the major groups. Hog bristles largely comprise the hard group and sable and squirrel hairs the soft.

bristle

Bristle brushes, always in plentiful supply, are seldom used in transparent watercolor painting. For the opaque processes, with the exception of egg tempera, bristle brushes are more amenable. Bristle brushes easily overcome the weight resistance of thickly prepared paints, and are capable of shoving and spreading impasto consistencies. But the stiffness of bristles can destroy transparent watercolors too easily during any phases of overlay painting; watercolor pigment, it may be recalled, clings lightly to the support surface and is easily disturbed. Stiff bristles tend to scrub, an action which loosens pigment grains. In fact, repeated vigorous scrubbing may cause loosening and rupture of the top layer of paper fibers. Painted areas thus mistreated become deadened with unsightly blemishes. Similar disintegration may occur while glazing in the egg tempera process. The scratching action of bristles drags unfixed pigment into erratically edged smearings which are almost beyond repair. If, however, it is intended that an area be eradicated or lightened in value range, light scrubbing with bristle brushes is helpful wherever water-soluble paints are used. On the positive side, the wider widths of bristle brushes are favored for scrubbing larger areas and for dry-brush effects.

sable

The resiliency of the softer sables is responsible for fewer faults than the bristle types. For this reason, and because finer hairs carry greater amounts of water and pigment, the sables are better attuned to watercolor manipulations. This ability to sustain large pigment loadings permits long strokes imbued with a wet and fresh color clarity. Strokes are clean and deft, varying easily from fine to broad because the buoyancy of sable hairs makes quick changes of pressure possible. The sables are so responsive to touch that they even convey some sense of human impulse and emotion, and produce a personalized calligraphy in many instances.

The best sables are made from the tail hairs of select species of Siberian mink. Unhappily, not even the prolific mink is able to keep pace with the enormous demand for its pelt. Consequently squirrel tail hairs have been compromised into a serviceable substitute which accounts for the bulk of commercial soft brushes. Incidentally, squirrel and so-called camel's hair brushes are one and the same. Within the sable group, sable and camel varieties may be distinguished by appreciable price differences; aside from cost, the mink is easily recognized by its reddish yellow color, which contrasts with the invariable red to gray and black gradations of squirrel hairs.

BRUSH SHAPES

In both the bristle and sable classes, the most common shape is the pointed tip, followed by flat, round, and domed. The domed brush is known in watercolor painting as a *wash brush*. Flared outward at the tip, the charged wash brush sweepingly covers greater surface areas with the aid of large amounts of water added during successive strokes. Gradated effects are achieved by this sable brush, but unfortunately the full effectiveness of the wash brush seems to have degenerated to the exclusive task of rendering skies. For this reason, the term "sky brush" is fairly prevalent. It is just such limited association of brush and function that establishes stereotyped usages. The same general criticism applies to the other brush modifications which constitute an auxiliary category. Among these, the fan, so called because of its shape, is assigned to the executing of foliage and hair. Surely it, together with other overly specialized designs, can be used with more imagination.

The stroke characteristics of the remaining brush shapes are fairly obvious. Pointed and round tips favor linear markings while the flat-sided tip lends itself to broad strokes. In choosing watercolor brushes, at least one each of the larger sables (Nos. 6, 8, 12) should be selected to provide a versatile core. The value of smaller sized brushes is dubious, since the better brushes can be made to produce the finest of strokes independently of size. There is hardly the minutest of indications which cannot be achieved by even the largest pointed sable. Smaller brushes too frequently lead to finicky and unstimulating techniques.

SIZE

Brush sizes are coded in numerical designations, from 000 to 8 in the French scale and from 0 to 12 in the Standard English. In both systems the largest flat brush, measuring across the ferrule edge, is approximately one inch in width. In spite of standardized calibration, there are deviations among brushmakers. The tufts of individual brands will vary in width, fullness, and length even though the numerical size is the same in each case. If at all possible, examine and compare brushes at retail supply houses, and heft them for their weight and feel in the hand. Beginners in particular should resist packaged sets of brushes and paints purchased with the trusting assumption that this procedure takes care of selection once and for all. Personal judgment proves more satisfying in the end. As for the advice of non-artist salespersons, be astute enough to realize that few of them know any more about brushes in general than is conveyed in the information on packages and in advertisements.

ORIENTAL BRUSHES

No review of watercolor implements can exclude brushes from the Orient. The exquisite calligraphy and economy of statement present in paintings of the Far East have elevated simplicity and directness of notation into a major watercoloring tenet. On the other hand, blind admiration for these qualities has mesmerized otherwise intelligent persons into the foolish supposition that the mere use of these same tools will magically summon a Chinese painting with all of its subtleties. If anything is to be extracted from a traditional form, such as the Chinese, let it be a creative philosophy and a cross-cultural understanding. Oriental brushes differ from western in both appearance and materials used; in structural principle there is no basic difference, however. Effects associated with tuft shapes are typical of the oriental brush types. Small pointed brushes of deer hair, for instance, are reserved to trace the veining of a leaf. A bamboo handle mounted with chicken feathers is reserved for still another time-honored effect, as are brushes made with fox and other wild animal hairs. The more common brushes, large by western standards, employ hog bristle and goat hair. Shaped to a point, these are actually writing brushes. The *Shodo Hokoku*, illustrated on page 11 are typical. These are used for executing large strokes as well as for covering wide areas. The largest size has a diameter of 1⅛ inches and 4¼ inches hair length. The smallest is ½ inch in diameter and 2 inches in length. They are made from horse hair and wool. The *hake*, or flat brush, is made from horse hair and is available in three sizes. The large is 3 inches wide with a hair length of 1¼ inches. The medium size is 2 inches wide, with a length of 1¼ inches also. The small is 1 inch wide and 1 inch long. These brushes are used for applying background color to wide areas, and hold a full charge of paint. They are also used to stretch rice papers. One group of standard brushes is associated with watercolors. These are called coloring brushes (Bunkan Saishiki). Five sizes are available.

SUPPLEMENTARY EQUIPMENT

Not all of the possible effects can be coaxed from the brushes discussed up to this point. A miscellany of odd brushes from the bargain counters of the five-and-dime stores and from the kits of sign-painters, house-painters, wallpaper hangers, and the plasterer for good measure, may be bizarre, but disassociation of tools from traditional functions provides a fruitful resource. Although the qualities of the softer brushes are sacrificed, more peculiarly appropriate effects of broadness, boldness, and outsized paintings may be achieved.

Felt-tipped tools are also useful. Some are indelible, and these will be found useful as resists with watercolors; other felt-tip pens, made expressly for sketching purposes, carry water-soluble inks. These prove more harmonious with watercolors. Still other uncommon results are within the range of possibility. Some painters hand-fashion brushes tailored to better convey the spirit of image to be represented. Wielding a brush fashioned from the chest hair of a pet collie can be unexpectedly pleasurable.

PUPPY-DOG TAILS

The experience exploring the capabilities of brushes can lead to some extemporaneous manipulation of commonplace materials. The whole problem of applying pigments can be re-created or relived, so to speak, by turning for a moment to improvised implements reminiscent of the forerunners of the brush. Match-sticks, cotton-tipped swabs, frayed rope, unraveled string, slivers of wood and bamboo might be dragged, dabbed, and scribbled anew, to extend the awareness of tool diversity and imaginative treatments. Strips of cardboard, steel-wool, crumpled paper, and cloth wadding might also come into play to achieve other graphic dimensions. Combinations and outcomes are potentially fruitful, but unfortunately an aura of novelty for its own sake is too often attached. "Painting" with a stick or a tuft of cotton becomes a meaningless activity unless the markings produced are related to specific ends or results.

HOLDING THE BRUSH

Brushes should be held firmly but not tightly lest flexibility in wielding and freedom of motion be drastically hampered. Above all, the manner of gripping a pencil or a pen for writing should not be transferred into a brush habit. Useful in overcoming the tendency toward too tight a grip is the Chinese practice of holding the brush above the ferrule, perpendicular to the plane of the support, and gripping it with the thumb and fingers as would be possible only while also holding an egg in the palm of the hand.

Different ways of holding the brush will be found to satisfy different purposes. Varying the direction in which the strokes are executed allows the brush to show more of itself: downward, upward, from left to right, from right to left, diagonally, and even erratically. The least exciting paintings are so often those which have been built in short side-to-side strokes, with no more characterization than comes from the covering of a wall or a fence with paint. Slap the brush against the panel. Roll it and drag it on its side. To bring his tools into greater play, painter John Marin is said to have held a brush in one hand and charcoal or a second instrument in the other, working each simultaneously in ambidextrous coordination.

THE CARE OF BRUSHES

Because they are expensive, good brushes should not be neglected or otherwise carelessly treated. Reshape the tips of sable watercolor brushes before putting them away. There are two ways to do this. Make sure that the brush is absolutely clean, and draw the tuft between the lips several times, working it into shape with saliva. Because of the remote chance that the brush might have retained some trace of poisonous color, most artists snap the brush downward several times instead; the hairs fall back into position by the sudden and violent ejection of water. Be reminded that only good brushes will respond in this way.

Brushes should not be permitted to stand on end unsupported for any length of time. When in storage, hanging or horizontal rest prevents deforming of hairs and shape. While painting, brushes left to stand in the rinsing container will sag likewise. In addition, the finish from the handle will flake off, causing the handle not only to swell but also to pry itself loose from the ferrule. The ferrules should be kept free of paint hardenings.

Sable brushes will lose shape badly if mistreated. However, they can be salvaged by dipping them in stand oil and reworking them into shape after the oil has begun to set. Some days later a washing in lighter-fluid will remove the oil; this should be followed by a washing with mild soap and tepid water.

India inks tend to stiffen brushes and affect their shaping. One solution to this problem is to use expendable brushes for inks. Insoluble inks, particularly the loose refill inks used for certain felt-tip fountain pens, are extremely difficult to dissolve from brushes.

Sable brushes are best kept in mothballs and covered in a cool place. Another method of protection is dipping the brush into camphorated oil, which seals the tuft under a coat of camphor when the alcohol evaporates.

In summary, to select a good brush, check it for elasticity, for a point that is soft and fine, and for a belly which will hold sufficient water to keep the point wet. The elasticity of a brush is judged by its ability to resume its shape and straighten out naturally. For a practical test of a sable brush, roll a brush which has been wetted and shaken free of excess water into a point on the palm of the hand. A thin and scraggly point is indicative of a lifeless brush without bounce or spring.

To test a bristle brush, load it with water and hold it in a horizontal position. If the water flows to the handle, try another brush.

CHAPTER 7

On Water

Water is so familiar a substance that any lengthy discussion of it would seem hardly necessary. Because most water is safe to drink, it seems quite natural that it should be safe for all purposes. However, as a chemical compound, and as a bearer of other chemicals and bacteria, water becomes instrumental in the physical changes which affect paints and papers.

The purity of water has been long a factor of watercolor processes. To this day distilled water continues to be used in grinding pigments for egg tempera. Pigments themselves, it might be added, should be free of lime. In papermaking the presence of iron and manganese in the water lessens the lucidity and color of the paper and may also cause brown spots. Other spottings are caused by organic substances. In Japan papermaking operations are located high in the mountains, where the water is fresh and at its purest. Papers produced upstream are of the best quality; the further downstream the paper is made, the progressively lower its quality. Because fewer impurities are to be found in cold water, the making of paper by hand in Japan is a winter industry.

Modern-day tap water is fine for all of the ordinary demands of watercolor methods. Municipal water supplies are filtered and chemically purified. Depending upon local geology, water may be *soft* or *hard*. In regions where hard water is prevalent, the high incidence of minerals may be removed by any of several water softening processes. Demineralized water, 99.9995 per cent free of minerals and fluorides, is commercially available in addition to conventionally distilled water. Mineral removal by ionization is three times as effective as that achieved by distillation. Rain water, which is naturally neutral, is too easily overlooked as a source.

When painting, the water used for moistening paints, for wetting the paper, and for brush rinsing should be kept as clean as possible. Whenever convenient, large containers are advantageous for keeping water relatively clear for a longer time. Although brush rinsings discolor water quickly, lifeless pigments settle to the bottom of the water container so that if the container is a large one, water close to the surface will be usable longer. To extend the usability of water, more than one container may be used for a series of bucket-to-bucket rinsings. Separate containers may also be reserved for wetting and for color mixing. If phthalocynine colors are used, it would be wise not only to rinse the brushes used with them in a separate container but also to have a special mixing surface isolated from the regular palette. Whatever system is employed, change the water frequently during the course of painting.

When field trips are planned, make sure to take along an adequate supply of water. Have enough for painting needs, for personal use, and for emergency. Unless absolutely certain that clean water will be available on the site, take no chances. Even the least likely of brooks becomes polluted, very often because of detergent discharges. In the unlikely event that the watercolorist is without water, improvisation may prove to be the only expedient. Slushed snow, for instance, is not only a practical alternative in the winter, but is also capable of producing novel effects. As has already been mentioned, ice crystals freeze with pigment into exquisite traceries of color. One desperate day water drained from an automobile radiator appeared not to have done harm either to the painting or to the car when returned to the cooling system afterward.

The insistence of artists upon tools and materials of premium quality must also include water. There are too many instances in which impure water can do injury. With a due sense of craftsmanship, the wise watercolorist does not neglect to take water into thorough account.

CHAPTER 8

Framing

The framing of a completed watercolor is more
necessary to its protection than to its enhancement. Both
aspects, however, are important for a functional
and harmonious relationship between frame and painting.
In concept, framing is the problem of presenting
a work most effectively while providing for its physical survival.
Three structural elements are common to all watercolor
frames: the mat, the frame itself within which
the mat is inserted, and a pane of glass behind which the
mat is fitted. This combination is standardized for
good reason, since each part serves to overcome the
several kinds of damage to which watercolors
are most commonly prone. The practical value of these
basic framing units does not necessarily interfere

with their imaginative treatment. Design modifications are perhaps as numerous as variations in the works themselves. Most often, however, artists come to prefer a variation of a favorite design which has proved the most compatible with the stylistic orders developed by the artist. In every instance, the appropriate frame solution emphasizes the painting and allows it to dominate, without distraction and contradiction.

The selection of materials for frame construction will be specified below. It is important to bear in mind that sturdiness, high quality, and minimized weight are the essential considerations in the housing of a painting. This may be better undertsood as each framing element —mat, outside frame, and glass—is taken up.

THE MAT

Preparation of the mat is the first step in making a frame. To an extent the mat alone may be considered as a frame and, in fact, under a number of conditions it is sufficient. Where optimum protection is desirable, as during storage for a lengthy period, matting a watercolor is sufficient. It might be well to add in respect to storage that the old practice of placing the work in a well sealed box kept in an area low in humidity and with constant temperature is a reliable precaution. If a watercolor is to be displayed for a short time only, matting may be all that is necessary. Works accepted by a jury for a major exhibition are displayed behind glass according to the preferences of the sponsor. This may be with or without an outside frame.

The most familiar mat stocks are made of paper boards, often referred to as mat board, pebble board or by make, such as Crescent. They are available in a range of colors, but white and gray tones are suitable for most paintings. Since permanence is also important, boards high in rag content are recommended. As they age, pulp boards cause any paper covered by them to yellow. Boards come in single and double thicknesses.

The cut mat is nothing more than a border surrounding an opening, and is known as the "window type" for obvious reasons. Centering of the opening, accurate cutting, and sufficient allowance of width for the border surrounding the opening make for a proper mat. Ragged and skimped jobs are unattractive, although narrow borders may be necessary with large paintings to reduce the weight and the size and thickness of the glass. For paintings of average size, side and top borders approximately three inches wide and of three-and-a-half to four inches along the bottom will be found workable. Any modifications of these dimensions, of course, should be made to complement the painting. Eventually one seems to sense the appropriate widths of borders for individual paintings. Aesthetically, painting and board make a rectangle within rectangle relationship.

A rule, a metal T-square, and any of the heavier razor-type knives available from art supply houses and hardware counters are needed for cutting a mat. If expense is not a factor, equipment designed for mat cutting is worth the difference in results for most people. When the perimeter around the painting has been decided, the size of the window is determined. Adding the widths of the borders to the size of the window yields the overall size of the mat. The paperboard is trimmed to this last size carefully, using the T-square and passing the knife with an even pressure several times in the line of the cuts. The knife should slice through the paper layers of the board cleanly. Forcing the blade with a single heavy pressure makes a tearing cut and, should the knife veer, may damage the board and perhaps a finger.

When the shaping of the mat is completed, the window is lightly penciled into place. At each corner the point of the knife is carefully worked into the board in the direction of each cut making incisions half an inch long. These scorings mark the start and the end of each of the border cuts which are made from corner to corner. Accidental slipping of cuts beyond the corners of the window is thereby prevented. Place the T-square so that it covers the mat border along the line of the cut to be made so that, should the knife skew, it will skew into the area of the window opening. Mat boards dull cutting tips and edges rather quickly, and the blade should be frequently replaced or sharpened with a flat slip stone. While cutting a mat, place a piece of clean paper or cloth beneath the free hand wherever it is placed on the board to prevent perspiration and body oils from staining the surface.

CUTTING A MAT

1.   The cutting of mats is not difficult. Needed will be a sharp cutting blade, such as a utility knife, shown here being sharpened; a soft, well pointed pencil; a metal yardstick or a wooden rule and a straight and even-edged length of metal; some fine sandpaper, and an eraser.

2.   A piece of pebble board has been carefully measured for its window. At each corner the board has been notched with the matting or utility knife. This will act as a stop which will help to keep the longer cuts from going beyond the corners of the window. Here a straight-edge is shown in place, on the margin side of the guideline. It is held steadily and cutting is achieved by several passes of the blade. A cleaner cut will result if only a few layers of the board are cut at a time, instead of by one cut under heavy pressure. If the knife should slip, with the straight-edge positioned as shown, the mat border would not be damaged.

3. The first cut completed, the board is turned to get it into position for the second cut. The board pictured here is the cutout from the window of a mat for a larger painting. Save cutouts for small watercolors or for the matting of prints.

4. Three sides of the window completed, the last cut is shown being made. Again, follow guidelines with the straight-edge covering the mat border and with the knife along the edge facing the window. The straight-edge used here is a section of aluminum channeling. It is quite sturdy, light, and does not warp.

5.   Slight ridges along the edges of the window can be felt as a result of the cutting. These come from pressures exerted upon the knife and from the thickness of the blade itself as it forces its way through the mat board. They can be worked down by light sanding. Often the corners need additional dressing, and this can be done with sandpaper also. Pencil marks should be lightly erased. If there are smudges, as from dust or careless handling, wipe the whole mat with a damp sponge. This will not harm the board and will avoid damage to the mat's surface which may result from too hard use of erasers.

Holding the knife at a right angle to the paper while cutting along each side produces a window with edges perpendicular to the painting. Single thickness stocks are ordinarily cut in this way. Another popular style of cutting is to bevel the opening. To achieve this style of cut, the knife is tilted at an angle as it rests against the edge of the T-square, then drawn firmly along several times until each cut is complete.

Before fitting the watercolor behind the completed mat, remove pencil marks and any other smudges with a soft eraser. Rub lightly and whisk off eraser crumbs with a soft brush or cloth. Irregularities and fuzziness anywhere along the cuts may be removed by gently scraping with fine sandpaper.

If necessary, the watercolor should be trimmed to a size close to that of the window, with variations of a few inches possible. Experts at restoration recommend that the painting be hinged only at the upper corners with paper tape, not along all the edges. Affixing a painting along only one edge allows it to expand and contract with varying humidity. The painting may then be safeguarded from abrasive damage by slipping a sheet of paper behind the mat to cover the window.

Cloth covered mats are employed frequently enough to be included in this discussion. Any mat of paper board may be covered with fabric easily. A full piece of cloth, such as muslin or linen, is cut slightly larger than the mat, and a rectangle slightly smaller than the window is cut from its center. Pasted to the mat with wheat paste, the cloth is lapped over the outside edges and those of the window. Smooth and even the cloth on the front and behind the mat and let it dry. When dry, any excess paste on the surface of the cloth is scarcely noticeable.

COVERING A MAT WITH CLOTH

1. A piece of linen, about two inches larger on all sides than the mat to be covered, is checked for fit.

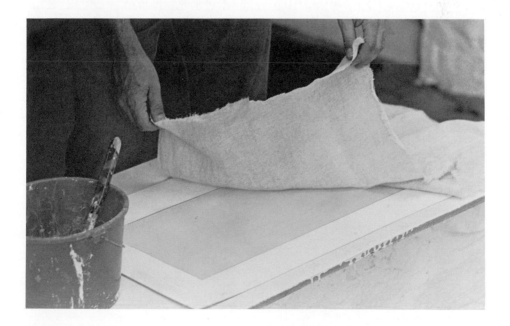

2. Paste, such as wheat (wallpaper) paste, has been applied to the mat's surface. With at least a three-inch brush, the cloth is evened and laid down. Here the brush has been wetted with water to aid the laying and to darken the area for the camera.

3. The window of the cloth is cut out. The opening will be smaller than that of the window. The darkened areas mark the outlines of the mat.

4.   With the center of the cloth cut away, a slit is made at each corner, the first step before the cloth overhang is turned under the inside edges of the mat.

5.   The mat is turned, cloth side down, and the turning under and the pasting down of the cloth overhangs are begun. Keeping the weave even, and very little pulling and stretching will lead to the most satisfactory results.

6.   The cloth is trimmed at the outside corners of the mat. When the cloth is turned under to the back, there will be no overlapping or bunching of cloth.

7.   The cloth should be fitted to the window corners before turning it down along all of the edges of the mat. Pressing into the corners is done with the dull edge of the scissors in this sample.

An important function of any mat is to isolate the watercolor from direct contact with glass when installed in a full frame. "Foxing," a type of injury to the painting from moisture which may condense behind the glass, is thereby forestalled. Furthermore, the adhesive strength of pigments tends to lessen under humid conditions.

If the cutting of a mat presents too many problems, pre-cut mats are available in standard sizes and designs. Many framing shops also provide cutting services.

THE GLASS

Glass is made in sheets of two basic thicknesses, 1/16", called single strength, and 1/8" or double strength. The difference in the weight is a factor in selecting glass for framing. Single-strength glass should be the first choice, of course, because with double-strength glass not only is the weight of the glass doubled, but also its cost. In framing small and average-sized works, single-strength glass is always easy to procure. With pieces larger than thirty-six inches on one edge, one is frequently obliged to settle for double-strength glass. The maximum dimension of single-strength glass is not thirty-six inches, however. Indeed, larger pieces in nonstandard shapes can be found, with sides reaching as much as thirty-six, forty, fifty-two, sixty and even seventy-two inches. But the extreme care necessary in handling these larger sizes makes them rather rare. Single strength glass will sag easily just from its own weight, and it will break just as easily for the same cause. Most sellers of glass would rather not stock single-strength glass in the larger shapes, but it can be specially ordered.

When ordering glass it is best to take the frame to the place where glass is sold. Let an expert measure, cut, and fit the glass. If there is any kind of variance in the frame, the glass may be cut to conform. Allow the glass to be slightly smaller than the frame's opening, to keep it from fitting too snugly and to avert breakage caused by forcing it into position. If the frame is made of wood, look for splinters and frayings from saw cuts. Remove these with a pocket knife or a sharp flat wood chisel. If the glass is slightly too large for the frame, the inside channels may be shaved with a chisel.

Glass reflects like a mirror, and misgivings are often expressed about this feature. A slight tilting forward of the frame picture reduces the amount of glare, and it is possible to design a frame which provides such a tilted set to the glass. Nonglare glass or varnishing are other possibilities. The first of these eliminates glare but it also imparts an oddly dull covering. And it is costly. The practice of varnishing watercolors has been raised as a question for several centuries. In spite of strong arguments against it, opinions favoring varnishing have prevailed to the extent that it has become a part of traditional painting procedures. A number of formulas for water varnishes may be found in the literature of other eras. In fact, varnishes were preferred to glass in England during the late eighteenth and the early nineteenth centuries. These varnishes were supposedly secret formulas, but they were all solutions of resinous substances in various solvents, such as alcohol, the essential oils of turpentine, lavender, etc. Tingry's "Varnisher's Guide" was the authoritative source for varnishes of the day. Some modern painters spray their work with acrylic solutions, in addition to glazing, and acetate sheets have also been tried in place of glass, but they become scratched and marred too easily.

For exhibition purposes, glass is generally specified as an entry requirement, although occasionally works need only to be matted. The probability of damage in transit is reduced if the glass is partly covered with strips of masking tape crossing one another. In case of an accident, broken sections of glass will be held by the tape, a protection both to the painting and to whoever unpacks the crate. Because of these problems, express companies and museums recommend that lucite be used instead of glass.

THE FRAME

The most common material for frames is wood. It is strong and available in various sizes, kinds, and forms. It is not difficult to shape and to modify generally. Traditionally almost every problem of framing has been solved with wood. Occasionally metal is used, but not too often.

Every lumberyard carries an assorted supply of preshaped mouldings which meet the particular needs of the building construction trade and also prove a ready source for frame-working. The simplest styles are the most practical. If more personalized shapes are preferred, these can be milled to order. When planning the frame, provide for sufficient depth and thickness to hold glass, mat, painting, and backing. The larger the painting, the heavier the stock must be to bear the weight.

The assembling of wooden frames is simple enough to be done at home with basic hand tools, but greater accuracy and a saving of time can be realized at a very small cost if a craftsman constructs the frame. The choice of finish can be left to the artist. Structurally substantial frames are mitered or dovetailed at the corners, glued under clamp, and additionally tightened with finishing nails. Unless you are reasonably adept with tools, assign the job to better hands.

FRAMING A WATERCOLOR

1. Using the frames to hold the glass, the glass is carefully cleaned and wiped with a lint-free cloth. The channel of the frame should be checked for stray matter, such as splinters or wood shreddings.

2.   Glass cleaned, the mat is lowered into the frame. Again, check for loose particles, for places missed on the glass, and be certain the mat is clean.

3.   The painting is placed behind the mat. The painting is mounted to masonite here, which will be the backing for the picture.

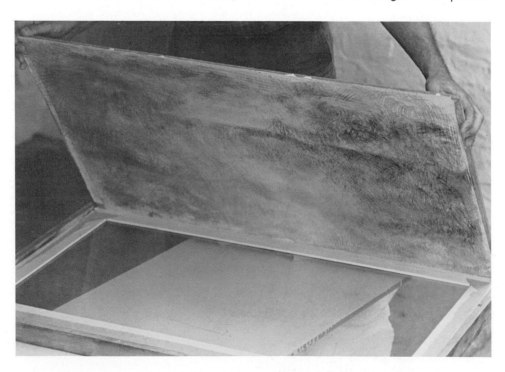

4.   The glass, the mat, and the painting in place within the frame, they are secured from behind by nails driven into the wood frame. Glazier's points are very convenient. Though not shown here, it is always a good idea to butt the frame against something immovable when hammering against each side.

5.   Clean the glass on the outside. The finish for this frame was achieved by scorching, wire-brushing, and grey paint wiped into the grain.

When frames are not elaborate, finishing the surfaces is simpli-fied. Finishes, like the frames, take their cue from the painting, especially in color and texture. The finish may be clean and trim, or it may be rough-hewn and rugged.

Raw wood is the simplest finish, but a light coat of clear varnish, diluted shellac, or wax will give some protection as well as a slight sheen when rubbed with fine sandpaper or steelwool. If colora-tion is desired, the raw wood may be stained with clear watercolors, gouache, or caseins. Wax stains are very successful. Gold leaf, if you can afford it, is a good companion for some, but not all, paint-ings. Gold leaf only was specified during watercolor's heyday in nine-teenth-century England. Gold and silver paints and synthetic "leaf" are too tawdry and garish to consider, even for a moment.

Frames may be textured by carving, by building-up gesso reliefs, and by other means just short of abusive. Wood has been rasped, scratched, pounded, drilled, and even scorched with flame to achieve effects. The last, done with a gas torch, raises the grain of the wood by burning out the softer cellular matter. A frame which has been wire-brushed and toned with ordinary water or oil paints—usually a gray—lends itself well to most landscape paintings. By the same token, still life and portraiture seem best with more formal designs.

Screw-eyes and picture wire will support most watercolors for hanging, but if the wood of the frame is soft and/or the weight is great, screw-eyes may pull loose. One excellent way of providing an anchoring in such cases is to rivet flat mirror-hooks to a piece of 1/8" masonite which is then fitted behind the painting. It will serve as a backing and the frame, bearing the glass, can be hung around it. Since the load is carried by the masonite, it becomes possible to use thinner and narrower framing stocks. When selecting hooks and wires, always be certain of their weight limits, which are in-variably indicated on the packaging. Two wall hooks will withstand the weight of glazed paintings better than one. They will also help the painting to hang straight.

Watercolors done on the lighter papers do not always lie flat, even when pressed by the mat and glass from the front and by the backing from behind. In recent years some painters have been successful in mounting works on illustration board panels, with dry-mount tissue and heat, in the same manner that photographs are adhered to a backing. Wrinkles or creases cannot always be prevented, however. Rubber cements have been used for evening the paper, but they, too, are not satisfactory because of a definite tendency to yellow the painting's surface. An old method popular during the days of Constable and Turner serves as well now as then. This mounting is described as follows.

Sponge both sides of three sheets of drawing paper, each a little larger than the intended mount; if they are rolled up while wet, the moisture will be evenly absorbed after a few minutes. Lay one of the sheets on a strong, smooth board, such as masonite, and turn up the edge of each side about an inch. Apply paste to these edges and press them down to the board. Library paste or vegetable glue will be satisfactory.

Shorten a second sheet about an inch in length and width. Place it down upon the first, centering it. Turn up one half of this second sheet, cover it evenly with paste, and lay it down again gradually, so as to drive the air before it without leaving bubbles. A wetted wide brush can be used to ease down the paper and to displace air, just as in the stretching of rice papers. The other half of the sheet is raised, pasted over, and laid down in the like manner. The third sheet is also shortened and laminated like the second. To avoid breaking of the mount or warping of the supporting board, the sheets should not be stretched to their fullest.

Trimmed to its final size, the drawing or painting is placed face downward on a clean piece of paper. Paste is spread and worked across its back and then allowed a short time to soften the support. In two or three minutes, according to the strength and thickness of the paper used for the painting, it can be laid with the pasted side to the mount and a clean sheet of paper over it to prevent injury from the rubbing necessary to fix it. If any air bubbles have appeared on taking up the paper from the face of the drawing, the end nearest to them must be raised up to allow them to escape. Very useful for this purpose are two straight pieces of wood, longer than the width of the drawing, covered with baize or flannel. By holding the paper down with one of these and passing the other over the paper on the face of the drawing, the air will be driven out better than it can be done by hand.

When the mounting has dried for several days it can be detached from the board by slitting it free within the pasted edges of the first sheet. Place the mounted work under some flat surface or within a portfolio to keep it flat while it continues to contract, no matter how dry it may seem to be.

Allowed a few more days, or even weeks, the painting may be taped by its top edge to another supporting board behind a mat. If all sides are taped down, the paper will not expand and contract if humid conditions exist. This instruction is also true, incidentally, for art prints.

Some painters like to present their paintings pasted down in another way. Instead of the mounting papers, linen or muslin is used to cover the whole mounting board. After the painting or drawing is adhered, the uncovered cloth serves, in effect, as an enframement in place of a mat. In lieu of the usual mat, two rabbeted channels may be cut into the frame stock, one for the glass and one for the painting and its mounting. In this way the painting surface is kept from coming into direct contact with the glass and the possibilities of the unhappy consequences explained earlier are avoided.

Framing, well and tastefully done, truly adds to the pleasure and enjoyment of a painting's mood.

In Conclusion

"Let go, thyself, and let God act for thee."
                    ANONYMOUS, *thirteenth century*

Painting techniques and philosophies began with water paints. Colored mud and clay on rock, hide, and body revealed to man his capacity to be an originator of form and imagery. Imagination was unlocked and individuality realized through simple means and relationships. Somewhere when someone struck a line of color with a chunk of mud, charcoal, or an attractive mineral, artistic expression was born. Learning to portray things outside himself, man became himself—the visionary, the artist and poet touching other men with love for the beautiful.

The simple means of the beginning moved into more complex procedures and relationships governing materials. Development of newer and more sophisticated meanings influenced refinements of technique, including the introduction of other media having water

191

as their vehicle. A succession of traditions have followed, some survive and others decline and become lost in the shadows of obscurity. Retracing the highlights of watercolor methods has been one of the tasks here. A surprising number of sound practices appear to have been neglected or forgotten, willfully perhaps, but more probably as the victims of other emphases. The passage of generations thrusts new values to the forefront, purging the old, all too often indiscriminately. Fortunately, a sufficient interest in things past persists to unite past and present in a perspective with the future.

Knowledge of art and its processes of themselves will not make an artist of the possessor. Awareness of craftsmanship and the behavior of materials are helpful, indeed, for the longevity of the work. Certain skills, too, such as the assuming of physical control of a medium, are useful. But the most important need is for the entrance of the self into an exchange with materials and equipment by which both man and means emerge mutually articulate, and even eloquent. The ancient Chinese painter described this relationship as the bringing together of "heart and hand." The real mission of technical growth, then, is to serve and convey imagery sensitively and selectively.

Some information compiled in this volume may seem to have been stressed more than other parts, but the author believes that the substance of each medium was reviewed as completely as necessary to enable one to approach it with least difficulty. Many painters, too, tend to fall out of touch with the tools and materials of their craft, taking too much for granted and becoming overly dependent upon their suppliers for assistance. On this point the real interest at heart throughout has been for the plight of students—young Turks, bless them—who always complain about not having been taught enough.

"Man is free to act, but must act to be free."

JEAN-PAUL SARTRE

Index

195